A

ADVENTURE

Script, Artwork and Colours: FRANCIS BERGÈSE

MISSING IN ACTION

The adventures of "Buck Danny" were created by Georges Troisfontaines, Victor Hubinon and Jean-Michel Charlier.

9th CINEBOOK
The 9th Art Publisher

Original title: Buck Danny 52 – Portés disparus
Original edition: © Dupuis, 2008 by Bergèse
www.dupuis.com
All rights reserved
English translation: © 2017 Cinebook Ltd
Translator: Jerome Saincantin
Editor: Erica Olson Jeffrey
Lettering and text layout: Design Amorandi
Printed in Spain by EGEDSA
This edition first published in Great Britain in 2017 by
Cinebook Ltd
56 Beech Avenue
Canterbury, Kent
CT4 7TA
www.cinebook.com
A CIP catalogue record for this book
is available from the British Library
ISBN 978-1-84918-343-7

WWRRRRRRR

CHOCOLATE MOUNTAIN AERIAL GUNNERY RANGE, SOUTH-EASTERN CALIFORNIA...

WWRRROOARRR

WWROOAARR

WWRRROOO

RAIDER TWO, RAIDER LEADER. ONCE WE EXIT THE CANYON, TAKE HEADING 150 TOWARD YUMA AND CLIMB TO FLIGHT LEVEL 60. THAT'S ENOUGH FOR TODAY, BOYS!

TWO WEEKS WE'VE BEEN MESSING AROUND IN THESE MOUNTAINS, PRACTICING TACTICAL FLIGHT AND CARGO DROPS!... HOW MUCH LONGER DO YOU THINK THIS'LL TAKE, BUCK?

THAT INFO IS ABOVE MY PAY GRADE, OLD BUDDY... KNOWING YOU, THOUGH, I WOULDN'T BE SURPRISED IF YOU END UP MISSING THIS TIME YOU FIND SO UNBEARABLE!

WHAT DO YOU THINK, TUMB? ANY IDEA WHERE THEY PLAN ON SENDING US AFTER TRAINING?

NOT A CLUE, MY DEAR CINDY. WHICH IS PRECISELY WHAT THE EXCITEMENT OF VOLUNTEERING FOR A SPECIAL MISSION IS ALL ABOUT! IN THE MEANTIME, I JUST APPRECIATE THIS OPPORTUNITY TO TEAM UP WITH YOU.

52.2A

MARINE CORPS AIR STATION, YUMA, ARIZONA, 20 MINUTES LATER...

MY ORDERS ARE TO TAKE COLONEL DANNY AND HIS TEAM TO THE BASE COMMANDER'S OFFICE!

702

52.2B

I HOPE WE'RE FINALLY GOING TO FIND OUT WHAT THEY HAVE IN STORE FOR US!

YOU VOLUN-TEERED, AND YET YOU HAVEN'T STOPPED GRUM-BLING!

NUH-UH! BUCK'S THE ONE WHO VOLUNTEERED... THEN YOU WENT ALL 'SIR, YES SIR!' AND FOLLOWED SUIT WITHOUT BATTING AN EYELASH!... WHAT WAS I SUPPOSED TO DO WITHOUT YOU GUYS?... YOU LEFT ME NO CHOICE!

WHAT ABOUT YOU, CINDY? WHY ON EARTH DID YOU JOIN US?

THEY NEEDED FOUR VOLUNTEER PILOTS... ONE FOR ALL AND ALL FOR ONE! I WASN'T GOING TO LET YOU LEAVE WITHOUT ME!

52.2C

SEE THIS? AN AIR FORCE LEARJET... LOOKS LIKE WE HAVE A BIGWIG IN THE HOUSE, GUYS!

COME IN, GENTLEMEN.

I'M SORRY — COME IN, LADY AND GENTLEMEN!

!

THREE OF YOU KNOW ME ALREADY, BUT ALLOW ME TO INTRODUCE MYSELF TO THE LADY: I'M MAJOR GENERAL SCOTT, US AIR FORCE*, FROM THE SPECIAL OPERATIONS COMMAND OFFICE AT THE PENTAGON**.

*SEE GHOST SQUADRON AND NIGHT OF THE SERPENT.
**US ARMED FORCES HEADQUARTERS NEAR WASHINGTON, DC

YOU'VE ALL BECOME EXPERT TRANSPORT PILOTS AFTER TRAINING ON THE C-130 HERCULES — YOUR BIRD FOR YOUR NEXT MISSION...

THIS TOP-SECRET FILE CONTAINS ALL THE INFORMATION YOU NEED FOR SAID MISSION. I'M GOING TO HAND IT TO COLONEL DANNY, WITH WHOM YOU WILL STUDY IT. WHEN YOU DEPART TOMORROW, YOU WILL BRING IT TO THE BASE COMMANDER, WHO'LL DESTROY IT IN YOUR PRESENCE.

THE SHORT VERSION IS: I'M SENDING YOU TO AFGHANISTAN TO INVESTIGATE THE DISAPPEARANCE OF A CIA* AGENT.

!

*CENTRAL INTELLIGENCE AGENCY: CIVILIAN FOREIGN-INTELLIGENCE AGENCY

ALAN JENKINS — THAT'S HIS COVER — WAS INVESTIGATING ARMS TRAFFICKING BETWEEN AFGHANISTAN AND IRAN. ACCORDING TO HIM, TRANSPORTATION HAS TO BE TAKING PLACE BY AIR, SINCE THE ROAD NETWORK IS CONTROLLED BY AFGHAN AND ALLIED MILITARY FORCES*...

*THE ARMED FORCES OF A US-LED INTERNATIONAL COALITION THAT SUPPORTED THE AFGHAN GOVERNMENT IN ITS FIGHT AGAINST TERRORISM FROM 2001 TO 2014

HE NEEDED TO BE ABLE TO GO FROM AIRFIELD TO AIRFIELD FREELY, SO THE CIA CREATED A SMALL COMPANY, THE AMERICAN MIDDLE AIR TRANSPORT, THAT RENTED ITS SERVICES TO HUMANITARIAN AID ORGANISATIONS. AS A PILOT, JENKINS HOPED HE'D EVENTUALLY CROSS PATHS WITH A CREW INVOLVED IN THE TRAFFIC — OR EVEN BETTER, THAT HE'D BE RECRUITED FOR IT.

HE HASN'T BEEN HEARD FROM AT ALL IN THREE WEEKS. THE PLANE — A BUFFALO* — AND ITS CREW HAVE VANISHED. IF JENKINS IS STILL ALIVE, LAUNCHING AN OFFICIAL INVESTIGATION COULD DRAW ATTENTION TO HIM AND PUT HIM IN DANGER.

*DE HAVILLAND CANADA DHC-5

THEREFORE, THE FOUR OF YOU, UNDER FALSE NAMES, ARE GOING TO BECOME TRANSPORT PILOTS FOR A BRITISH COMPANY, THE LAP — LOWLAND AIR PARTNERSHIP — AND WILL CARRY OUT HUMANITARIAN AID DELIVERIES IN THE SAME AREA. TRY TO FIND OUT WHAT BECAME OF JENKINS, AND SEE IF YOU CAN UNCOVER SOME LEADS ABOUT THE ARMS TRAFFICKING TOO.

DON'T FORGET: ONCE YOU'RE IN AFGHANISTAN, UNTIL YOUR MISSION HAS BEEN COMPLETED, YOU WON'T HAVE ACCESS TO ANY KIND OF HELP. FORTUNATELY, YOU'LL HAVE TO PICK UP YOUR CARGO IN KARACHI, PAKISTAN. ONE OF OUR AGENTS WILL BE YOUR CONTACT THERE AND WILL KEEP US APPRISED OF YOUR MISSION PROGRESS...

UH... AND HOW ARE WE GETTING THERE, SIR?... WITH OUR C-130S?

NO, DON'T WORRY! FIRST YOU'LL BE TAKEN TO WASHINGTON BY MILITARY TRANSPORT...

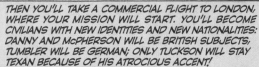

THEN YOU'LL TAKE A COMMERCIAL FLIGHT TO LONDON, WHERE YOUR MISSION WILL START. YOU'LL BECOME CIVILIANS WITH NEW IDENTITIES AND NEW NATIONALITIES: DANNY AND McPHERSON WILL BE BRITISH SUBJECTS, TUMBLER WILL BE GERMAN; ONLY TUCKSON WILL STAY TEXAN BECAUSE OF HIS ATROCIOUS ACCENT!

ME? AN ACCENT?! WHERE DID HE GET THAT IDEA?!

HA! HA! HA!

ANOTHER COMMERCIAL FLIGHT WILL TAKE YOU TO KARACHI...

I MEAN, I'D KNOW IT IF I HAD AN ACCENT!

HA! HA! HA!

52.4A

...WHERE YOU WILL FIND YOUR AIRCRAFT AND YOUR TEAM...

LOWLAND AIR PARTNERSHIP

...ONE FLIGHT ENGINEER AND ONE LOADMASTER PER PLANE. THEY'RE SPECIAL FORCES TRAINED TO FACE ANY SITUATION, AND THEY'RE FULLY AWARE OF THE MISSION'S OBJECTIVES...

DO YOU THINK I HAVE A TEXAS ACCENT?

ER...

HERCULES

52.4B

LOADED WITH HUMANITARIAN AID, YOU'LL TAKE YOUR PLANES TO QALA I NAW, AN AIRPORT IN NORTH-WESTERN AFGHANISTAN...

THERE, YOU'LL HAVE TO REPORT TO A GOVERNMENT OFFICIAL...

LOWLAND AIR PARTNERSHIP

HELLO! WELCOME TO QALA I NAW. IN THE NAME OF MY GOVERNMENT, I THANK YOU FOR YOUR HELP! I AM TO BE YOUR GUIDE...

52.4C

I'LL NEED THE TWO AIRCRAFT COMMANDERS TO COME WITH ME TO THE OFFICE FOR THE PAPERWORK.

GREAT! AND OFF THEY GO — WITHOUT US!... WELL, I'M NOT GOING TO JUST SIT HERE!

SHALL WE SNOOP AROUND THE HANGARS AND TRY TO FIND SOME CLUES ABOUT JENKINS' PLANE?

I'LL GO WITH YOU, BOB. JENNY, YOU SHOULD STAY HERE... THE PRESENCE OF A WOMAN — ESPECIALLY ONE NOT WEARING A HIJAB — COULD BE SEEN AS A PROVOCATION.

OK. LET'S GO, BART!

MY NAME IS ASIM.

I'M KENNETH HARRISON... CALL ME KEN!

I'M KARL... KARL STUMPFF!

I WILL BE TELLING YOU WHERE TO DROP OFF OR COLLECT THE AID PACKAGES. I'LL ALSO BE YOUR INTERPRETER.

WE HEARD ABOUT A PLANE DOING THE SAME JOB THAT VANISHED THREE WEEKS AGO... DID IT HAVE A GUIDE TOO?

52.5A

OF COURSE. THAT DAY, IT WAS SUPPOSED TO DO A DROP IN A SPECIFIC ZONE, BUT IT WASN'T SEEN THERE. THE SEARCH OPERATIONS TURNED UP NOTHING. ITS DISAPPEARANCE IS A COMPLETE MYSTERY!

خط هوایی بادغیس
BADGHIS AIR SYSTEM

THE LOCAL AIR COMPANY...

YEAH... THREE SOVIET-MADE AIRCRAFT, KINDA OLD!

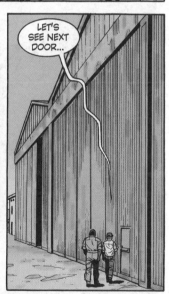

LET'S SEE NEXT DOOR...

IT'S LOCKED.

THE NEXT HANGAR OVER IS OPEN. LET'S GO!

52.5B

A CHOPPER AND SOME OLD CRATE!

THERE! IN THE BACK, NEAR THE OFFICES, THERE'S A DOOR TO THE LOCKED HANGAR... SHALL WE TAKE A LOOK?

OH!

A BUFFALO! THAT'S A STRANGE COINCIDENCE!... BUFFALOS ARE PRETTY RARE. I'D GO AS FAR AS TO SAY THAT UNTIL JENKINS ARRIVED, THEY'D NEVER SEEN ONE AROUND HERE...

IT LOOKS BRAND NEW... IT GOT A FRESH COAT OF PAINT RECENTLY.

THE REGISTRATION NUMBER IS AFGHANI...

WE'D NEED TO KNOW IF IT'S A RECENT REGISTRATION...

LOOKING FOR SOMETHING, GENTLEMEN?

52.6A

ER... NO!... JUST VISITING!

WELL, THIS IS PRIVATE PROPERTY!

SORRY. WE'VE GOT TIME TO WASTE, SO WE'RE DOING WHAT ALL FLIGHT CREWS DO IN SUCH CIRCUMSTANCES: WE GO EXPLORING!

AND WHAT WERE YOU WRITING DOWN? THE REGISTRATION NUMBER?

YEAH... SURELY THAT'S NOT A PROBLEM?... I HAVE A SPOTTER FRIEND — YOU KNOW, THOSE WACKOS WHO COLLECT REGISTRATION NUMBERS BY AIRCRAFT TYPES AROUND THE WORLD!

OH, YEAH! PLENTY OF GUYS LIKE THAT IN THE US, WRITING DOWN TAIL NUMBERS IN LITTLE NOTEBOOKS!

FINE... NOW GO BACK THE WAY YOU CAME FROM AND GET OUT!

ARE YOU AMERICAN?

SURE AM. AND SO ARE YOU, I BET... IN FACT, I'D SAY YOU'RE FROM TEXAS!

52.6B

8

YEAH! HOW DID YOU GUESS?

DOESN'T TAKE A GENIUS WITH AN ACCENT LIKE YOURS!

ARE THOSE C-130S THERE YOURS?... IF YOU'RE STAYING FOR A FEW DAYS, WE'RE BOUND TO MEET AGAIN — THIS PLACE ISN'T EXACTLY A BIG HUB. SEE YA!

WELL, HELLO... LOTS OF PEOPLE NEAR OUR PLANES!

WAIT A MINUTE... IT LOOKS LIKE THEY'RE TAKING OUR CARGO!

WHAT'S GOING ON HERE?

SALAAM ALAYKUM. I AM THE REPRESENTATIVE OF THE GOVERNOR OF THE PROVINCE. WE'RE HERE TO COLLECT THE SHARE THAT WILL GO TO THE CHARITABLE ORGANISATIONS OF QALA I NAW...

BUT THE REPRESENTATIVES OF THE CHARITIES IN KARACHI HAD ASSURED US WE'D TAKE PART IN THE DISTRIBUTION!

THAT'S RIGHT! I INSIST THAT ONE OF US STAY WITH THE CARGO UNTIL IT REACHES ITS INTENDED RECIPIENTS!

WHAT?... ARE YOU QUESTIONING THE INTEGRITY OF MAHMOUD JARKHAN, OUR GOVERNOR? THE LADY IS HOLDING THE REQUISITION ORDER HE HIMSELF SIGNED. IT ONLY REQUIRES THE AGREEMENT OF YOUR TEAM LEADER...

THERE'S NO MENTION OF WEIGHT, OF QUANTITY OF FOOD OR MEDICAL SUPPLIES... THIS REQUISITION IS COMPLETE NONSENSE! I CAN ASSURE YOU OUR TEAM LEADER WILL NOT SIGN THIS RAG... IN FACT, YOU'LL BE BETTER OFF USING IT FOR YOU-KNOW-WHAT!

YOU... YOU...

THERE'S OUR TEAM LEADER, KEN, NOW.

KEN! YOU WON'T BELIEVE WHAT'S GOING ON! THEY WANT TO SNATCH TWO TRUCK-LOADS OF GOODS FROM US!

YES, I'M AWARE.

THE AIRPORT DIRECTOR EXPLAINED EVERYTHING. NO PROBLEM! START UNLOAD-ING THE PLANES — WE'VE ALL WASTED ENOUGH TIME AS IT IS!

TWO HOURS LATER...

G-BCTZ

!?

WELL, THAT'S THAT. WE'RE DOWN TO HALF OF OUR SHIPMENT...I GUESS THE DISTRIBUTION WILL GO FASTER!

I'D LIKE TO KNOW HOW YOU FEEL ABOUT WHAT JUST HAPPENED, ASIM.

THE SAME WAY YOU DO, KEN... BUT REBELLING WOULDN'T HAVE ACCOMPLISHED ANYTHING, UNLESS BEING EXPELLED FROM THE COUNTRY WAS YOUR GOAL!

52.8A

WHAT I'M ABOUT TO TELL YOU IS NO SECRET, BUT NOT TALKING ABOUT IT OPENLY IS OFTEN A HEALTHIER PROPOSITION. MAHMOUD JARKHAN, THE GOVERNOR, IS AN ALL-POWERFUL WARLORD. THE CENTRAL GOVERNMENT IN KABUL HAS NO CHOICE BUT TO DEAL WITH HIM ... AS WELL AS MANY OTHERS IN OTHER REGIONS.

IT'S UNAVOIDABLE. CIVIL WAR IS STILL JUST BELOW THE SURFACE, AND IT WOULDN'T TAKE MUCH FOR IT TO FLARE UP AGAIN.

BADGHIS HOTEL
هتل بادغيس

I WISH YOU A GOOD STAY. I'LL BE BACK TO FETCH YOU TOMORROW AT EIGHT... THIS ENVELOPE CONTAINS THE DETAILS OF THE DELIVERIES WE MUST MAKE, WITH LARGE-SCALE MAPS OF THE RELEVANT AREAS.

THANKS, ASIM.

52.8B

BART, MAX, FRANKIE AND STEVE, YOU'RE FREE UNTIL ZERO EIGHT HUNDRED TOMORROW MORNING. KARL, JENNY AND BOB, COME JOIN ME IN MY ROOM ONCE YOU'RE SETTLED IN. WE'LL PREPARE FOR TOMORROW'S MISSION.

LATER...

I KNOW WHAT YOU'RE THINKING ABOUT WHAT HAPPENED AT THE AIRPORT, FOLKS... BUT AT LEAST IT GAVE YOU AN IDEA OF THE GENERAL MOOD AROUND HERE.

KEEP YOUR HEADS DOWN — THAT'S THE MOTTO... THE AUTHORITIES ARE ALWAYS RIGHT. MORE THAN THAT, ACTUALLY: IF THE AUTHORITIES WANT SOMETHING, CONSIDER IT AN ORDER. ONLY BY TOEING THE LINE WILL WE BE ABLE TO FULFIL OUR MISSION.

BUCK, I...

CALL ME KEN, BOB.

WHILE YOU WERE FILLING OUT FORMS WITH TUM... ER... KARL, BART AND I WENT TO TAKE A LOOK INSIDE THE HANGARS. WE FOUND A KHAKI-COLOURED BUFFALO THAT LOOKED LIKE IT HAD BEEN PAINTED VERY RECENTLY...

52.9A

JENKINS' BUFFALO WAS WHITE... DID YOU SCRATCH THE PAINT A LITTLE TO SEE IF THERE WAS ANOTHER LAYER UNDERNEATH?

WE WERE UNCEREMONIOUSLY KICKED OUT... DIDN'T PUSH OUR LUCK!

THE BUFFALO IS NOT A COMMON PLANE, THAT'S TRUE. ESPECIALLY NOT HERE, WHERE ALMOST ALL EQUIPMENT IS SOVIET-MADE. WE NEED A CLOSER LOOK AT THAT BIRD — AND SOME INFO ON ITS OWNER.

UNFORTUNATELY, AS SOON AS WE'VE DELIVERED OUR CARGO, WE'LL HAVE TO RETURN TO KARACHI TO PICK UP ANOTHER LOAD. WHICH ISN'T CONVENIENT, AS IT COULD COST OUR INVESTIGATION SEVERAL DAYS...

IN ORDER TO STICK AROUND, I'M GOING TO FAKE A MECHANICAL FAILURE TOMORROW ON THE RETURN FLIGHT. WHILE KARL AND HIS CREW RETURN TO KARACHI, AND BART AND FRANKIE PRETEND TO WORK ON THE PLANE, BOB AND I WILL KEEP LOOKING FOR A LEAD THAT MIGHT TAKE US TO JENKINS — DEAD OR ALIVE.

NOW LET'S STUDY OUR MISSION, AND THEN ... WE'VE ALL EARNED A DRINK. I'M BUYING!

52.9B

AN HOUR LATER...

CHEERS!

PROSIT!

YOU KNOW THAT GUY?

HE'S ONE OF THE TWO FELLAS WHO KICKED US OUT OF THE BUFFALO HANGAR. AN AMERICAN... AT LEAST HE SEEMS LIKABLE!

WHAT'S HE DOING HERE?

DUNNO ... BUT I'D LIKE TO... I'M GOING TO GO HAVE A LITTLE CHAT WITH HIM!

CAREFUL, OK? WATCH YOUR STEP.

COME ON, YOU KNOW ME: TACT AND SUBTLETY!

52.10A

CHEERS!

CHEERS, MY TEXAS FRIEND!

COME HERE, BUDDY, AND TELL ME WHAT BRINGS YOU TO THIS DUMP!

BUT FIRST, WHAT ARE YOU DRINKING? FIRST ONE'S ON ME!

UM... IT'S OK, I STILL...

D'YOU KNOW THAT IN THIS LAND OF THIRST, YOU CAN'T EVEN DRINK ALCOHOL?!... EXCEPT HERE, IN THE ONLY INTERNATIONAL HOTEL WITHIN A HUNDRED MILES!... SO YOU'VE GOTTA STOCK UP!

UH... WHISKY, THEN!

HEY! WE HAVEN'T BEEN PROPERLY INTRODUCED YET! MERVIN C. HUNTLEY, FROM TULSA, OKLAHOMA. THEY CALL ME EMCEE!

ROBERT S. BRADY, FROM DALLAS. CALL ME BOB!

BOB! MY NEIGHBOUR*!... MAN, AM I GLAD THAT I MET YOU!

*OKLAHOMA AND TEXAS SHARE A BORDER.

52.10B

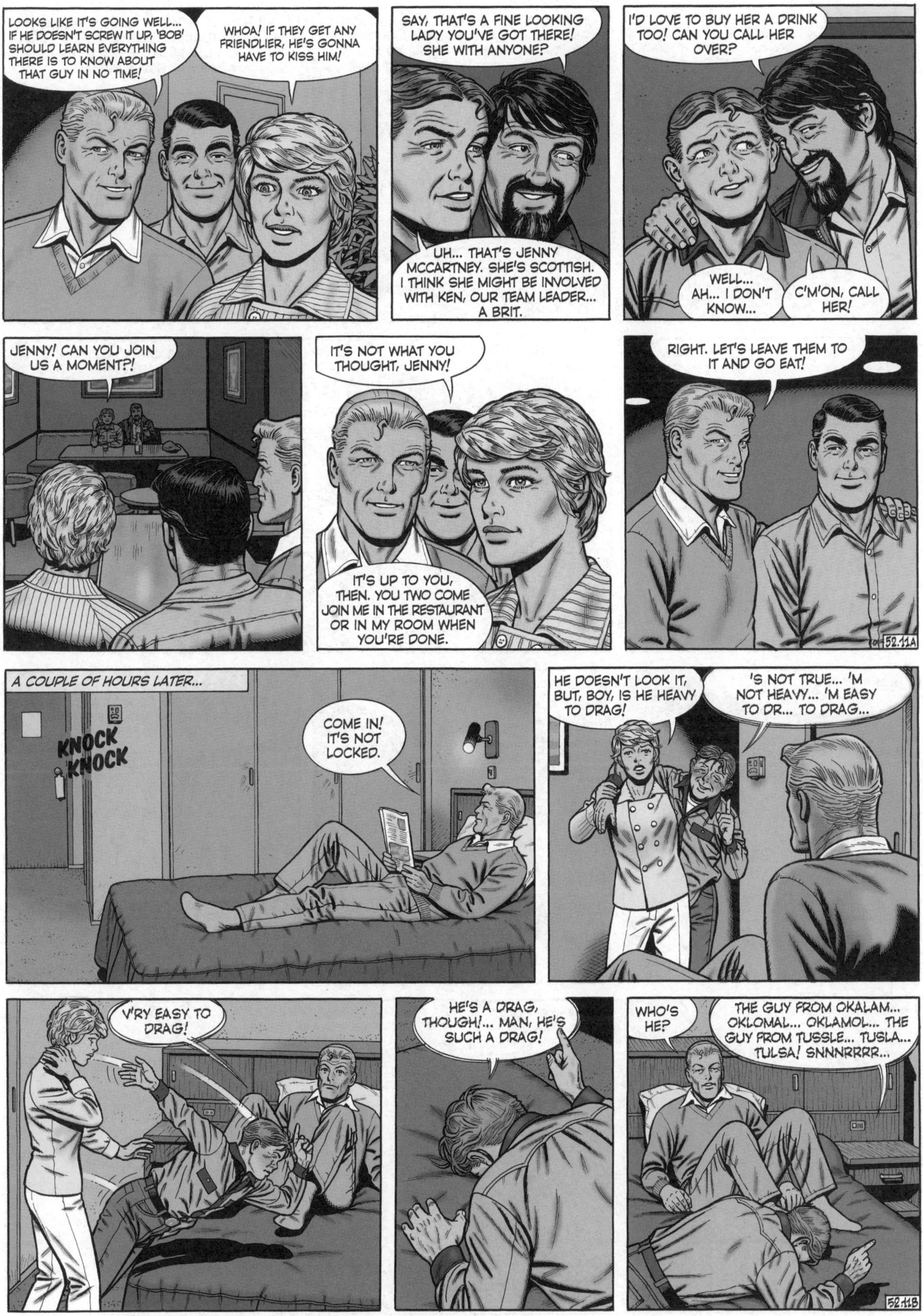
LOOKS LIKE IT'S GOING WELL... IF HE DOESN'T SCREW IT UP, 'BOB' SHOULD LEARN EVERYTHING THERE IS TO KNOW ABOUT THAT GUY IN NO TIME!
WHOA! IF THEY GET ANY FRIENDLIER, HE'S GONNA HAVE TO KISS HIM!
SAY, THAT'S A FINE LOOKING LADY YOU'VE GOT THERE! SHE WITH ANYONE?
UH... THAT'S JENNY MCCARTNEY. SHE'S SCOTTISH. I THINK SHE MIGHT BE INVOLVED WITH KEN, OUR TEAM LEADER... A BRIT.
I'D LOVE TO BUY HER A DRINK TOO! CAN YOU CALL HER OVER?
WELL... AH... I DON'T KNOW...
C'MON, CALL HER!
JENNY! CAN YOU JOIN US A MOMENT?!
IT'S NOT WHAT YOU THOUGHT, JENNY!
IT'S UP TO YOU, THEN. YOU TWO COME JOIN ME IN THE RESTAURANT OR IN MY ROOM WHEN YOU'RE DONE.
RIGHT. LET'S LEAVE THEM TO IT AND GO EAT!
52.11A
A COUPLE OF HOURS LATER...
KNOCK KNOCK
COME IN! IT'S NOT LOCKED.
HE DOESN'T LOOK IT, BUT, BOY, IS HE HEAVY TO DRAG!
'S NOT TRUE... 'M NOT HEAVY... 'M EASY TO DR... TO DRAG...
V'RY EASY TO DRAG!
HE'S A DRAG, THOUGH!... MAN, HE'S SUCH A DRAG!
WHO'S HE?
THE GUY FROM OKALAM... OKLOMAL... OKLAMOL... THE GUY FROM TUSSLE... TUSLA... TULSA! SNNNRRRR...
52.11B

PHEW! HE'S TANKED!

IT WAS CLEAR I WOULDN'T BE ABLE TO GET HIM TO TALK UNLESS BOB GOT HIM TO DRINK MORE — BUT OF COURSE HE HAD TO DRINK ALONG!

RESULTS?

INTERESTING... HE'S A PILOT FOR BADGHIS AIR SYSTEM, WORKING FOR AN IMPORT/ EXPORT COMPANY. AND THE OWNER OF BOTH IS ALSO THE OWNER OF THIS VERY HOTEL!

HE FERRIES GOODS, MOSTLY BETWEEN HERE AND TURKMENISTAN... HE'S OFFERED TO POACH US, BECAUSE HIS BOSS JUST BOUGHT A NEW AIRCRAFT...

HE DI'N'T SAY, BUT 'M SURE IT'S THAT BUFFALO! HOW'S THAT FOR A DRAG, HUH?... SNNNRRRR...

AND TO BAIT THE HOOK, HE ADDED:

OF COURSE THE PAY ISN'T THAT GREAT, BUT SINCE WE'VE GOT PLENTY OF DOWNTIME, WE CAN GO ABOUT OUR BUSINESS, AND ... FROM TIME TO TIME, THERE ARE SOME ... SPECIAL CARGOES ... THAT ARE WORTH SIZABLE BONUSES...

52.12A

HUSH, THOUGH... I DIDN'T SAY A WORD, OK?

WE HEARD... HIC!... NUTH'N'! CHEERS!

WE MIGHT BE INTERESTED, BUT WE NEED TO KNOW A LITTLE MORE...

YOU, GIRL, WILL HAVE TO START WITH WRAPPING YOUR HEAD IN A SCARF AND PUTTING YOUR HEADSET OVER IT ALL!

AT THAT POINT, IT SEEMED LIKE HE WAS BEGINNING TO REGRET WHAT HE'D SAID. BOB KEPT DRINKING WITH HIM, BUT THAT DIDN'T HELP.

HE AIN'T TOO SMART, THAT OKLAMO... OKLAHOMAHOMA... SNNNRRRR...

THANKS, CINDY. YOU CAN GO — I'LL GET SONNY BACK TO HIS ROOM.

AHHHH... CAREFUL, KEN, YOU'RE USING THE WRONG NAMES! SNNRRRRFF...

HA! HA! HA!

52.12B

14

THE NEXT DAY, SOME 100 MILES EAST, ABOVE THE NEIGHBOURING FARYAB PROVINCE...

THIS IS LOWLAND 1... WE'RE COMING UP ON OUR DROP POINT FOR SITE A, NEAR THE VILLAGE OF KUHESTAN.

THIS IS LOWLAND 2, FIVE MINUTES WEST OF OUR DROP POINT FOR SITE B, NEAR THE VILLAGE OF TEYLAN.

SWITCHING TO DROP CON-FIGURATION... OPENING CARGO DOORS... READY BACK THERE?

BART HERE. READY TO ROLL IT OUT, SKIPPER*!

*AIRCRAFT COMMANDER

WE'LL MAKE A PASS ALONG THE FOOTBALL FIELD... IT'S WIDE OPEN.

FIRST PACKAGE IS AWAY!

LOWLAND 1. DROP ON SITE A SUCCESSFUL.

THE CROWD IS BEING KEPT AWAY... IS THAT HOW IT'S SUPPOSED TO GO, ASIM?

LOWLAND AIR PARTNERSHIP

OF COURSE... IT IS THE ROLE OF THE AUTHORITIES TO COLLECT THE SHIPMENT AND DISTRIBUTE IT ACCORDING TO NEED.

I SEE... LET'S HEAD FOR MEYMANEH AIRFIELD NOW.

THIS IS LOWLAND 2. ON APPROACH TO SITE B. SWITCHING TO DROP CONFIGURATION.

A FEW MINUTES LATER, FURTHER NORTH...

LOWLAND 2... THE DROP WAS SUCCESSFUL. HEADING TOWARD MEYMANEH!

52.14A

ESTIMATED FLIGHT TIME: EIGHT MINUTES.

TWELVE MINUTES FOR US. DON'T WAIT FOR US — LAND AS YOU ARRIVE.

ACKNOWLEDGED, LOWLAND 1. SEE YOU SOON.

REMEMBER THAT MEYMANEH SEES SO LITTLE TRAFFIC THAT IT DOESN'T HAVE A CONTROL TOWER...

THE STRIP IS LONG, BUT IT'S DIRT... BETTER MAKE A PASS TO CHECK ITS CONDITION FIRST.

A FEW MINUTES LATER...

LOWLAND 1, LOWLAND 2. THE STRIP LOOKS ALL RIGHT... SLIGHT WIND FROM THE SOUTH-EAST... LANDING ON 32*... AVOID THE FIRST TWO OR THREE HUNDRED YARDS, THOUGH — THEY LOOK IN BAD SHAPE. THE WELCOMING COMMITTEE IS ON THE RAMP!

*A RUNWAY'S ALIGNMENT IS INDICATED IN DECADEGREES, ROUNDED TO THE NEAREST FROM ITS ACTUAL ORIENTATION. FOR EXAMPLE, A STRIP WITH A HEADING OF 076° WILL BE CALLED 08.

IT'S GOING TO BE JUST LIKE QALA I NAW, ISN'T IT?...

DON'T ROCK THE BOAT, BOB ... AS OUR FRIEND ASIM ADVISED!

I SEE YOU'RE BEGINNING TO FIT IN!

52.14B

A LITTLE LATER...

...SO THIS PLANE'S CARGO WILL GO INTO THIS TRUCK, AND THAT ONE INTO THE OTHER...

PLEASE SIGN THIS FORM.

AND WHO AM I ADDRESSING, SIR?

I AM THE ASSISTANT FOR SOCIAL AFFAIRS TO THE GOVERNOR OF FARYAB PROVINCE, AND THIS IS THE MAYOR OF MEYMANEH.

WOULD IT BE POSSIBLE TO ATTEND THE DISTRIBUTION?

I SEE NO REASON WHY YOU COULDN'T... HOWEVER, I DOUBT YOU'LL HAVE THE OPPORTUNITY: IT WILL TAKE TWO OR THREE DAYS TO TAKE STOCK AND ALLOCATE EVERYTHING ...

WILL THE FLIGHT CAPTAINS AND THEIR GUIDE HAVE TEA WITH US WHILE THEIR AIRCRAFT ARE UNLOADED?

IT'S ALL ABOUT THE BOSSES, HERE.

YOU DON'T EVEN LIKE TEA!

COME ON — I'LL BUY YOU A CUP OF COFFEE!

HEY! PROUD MOUNTAIN MAN!

I'LL TRADE YOU MY MAGNIFICENT CAP FOR YOUR NO-LESS-MAGNIFICENT BUT RATHER WEATHERED TRADITIONAL HAT!

I'LL EVEN THROW IN 5,000 AFGHANIS*!

*ABOUT US$1 AT THE TIME

A FEW MINUTES LATER...

...SO THERE YOU ARE, BART. WE COULDN'T TELL YOU BEFORE BECAUSE WHEN WE ALL MET IN THE HOTEL LOBBY THIS MORNING, ASIM WAS ALREADY THERE...

OK! WELL, GET READY TO WATCH HOW GOOD AN ACTOR AN ENGINEER CAN BE!

WE HAVE ABOUT AN HOUR... I NEED MY TOOLBOX AND A LADDER, AND I'LL COOK US UP A NICE LITTLE FUEL LEAK TO MAKE IT ALL MORE REALISTIC!

52.16A

AN HOUR LATER, THE CAR IS BACK AT THE AIRFIELD...

ONE OF YOUR MEN IS WORKING ON AN ENGINE... IS THERE A PROBLEM?

ER... YES... THAT ENGINE IS TEMPERAMENTAL. IT OCCASIONALLY LOSES THRUST...

I HADN'T NOTICED ANYTHING.

YOU KNOW, ON A FOUR-ENGINE KITE IT'S HARD TO TELL, UNLESS YOU HAVE YOUR NOSE ON THE GAUGES AND A TRAINED EAR!

YOU CAN MAKE THE RETURN TRIP WITH ME IF YOU PREFER.

OH, I'M NOT WORRIED!

I'D RATHER YOU DID, ASIM. JUST IN CASE...

52.16B

CARGO BAYS EMPTY, THE TWO C-130S ARE SOON FLYING BACK TO QALA I NAW...

THAT ENGINE IS SMOKING... THERE REALLY IS A PROBLEM!

LET'S HOPE IT'S NOT TOO SERIOUS. WE'RE NOT EQUIPPED FOR BIG REPAIR JOBS...

FROM INSIDE I COULDN'T SEE THAT SMOKE... I HOPE YOU'LL BE ABLE TO REPAIR IT!

WE'D BETTER, CONSIDERING ALL THE CARGO STILL WAITING FOR US IN KARACHI...

THIS IS LOW-LAND 1... THE ENGINE TEMPERATURE KEEPS CLIMBING... WE HAVE TO SHUT IT OFF.

52.16C

LOWLAND 1, LOWLAND 2. THE SMOKE IS THINNING.

AFTER ANOTHER 30 MINUTES IN THE AIR, THE AIRCRAFT ARE BACK AT THEIR BASE...

WHAT WILL YOU DO?

FIRST, OUR MECHANICS WILL TRY TO ASCERTAIN THE PROBLEM. IT MAY BE NECESSARY TO HAVE ANOTHER ENGINE SHIPPED IN AND TO SWAP IT WITH THIS ONE...

IN WHICH CASE, WE'LL HAVE TO CALL UPON THE GOODWILL OF WHOEVER OWNS THIS AIRFIELD'S REPAIR SHOP. AND IF THAT DOESN'T WORK OUT, WE'LL NEED TO TAKE THE PLANE TO KARACHI ON THREE ENGINES.

52-17A

THAT EVENING...

SO, TOMORROW KARL AND HIS CREW WILL GO BACK TO KARACHI TO PICK UP A NEW SHIPMENT.

BART, GET MAX TO HELP YOU REMOVE THE ENGINE CASING AND PARTS. ASIM AND I WILL GO REPORT OUR PROBLEMS TO THE AIRFIELD DIRECTOR.

WE DIDN'T SEE OUR FRIEND EMCEE AT THE BAR TONIGHT. IT MIGHT BE INTERESTING TO KNOW WHETHER HE FLEW TODAY, AND WHERE...

I'M ALSO CURIOUS TO KNOW IF THAT BUFFALO IS STILL HERE. BOB AND I WILL TAKE ADVANTAGE OF OUR FORCED DOWNTIME TO DO SOME INVESTIGATING...

YEAH ... EXCEPT WE'RE GONNA BE TRIPPING OVER ASIM!

BEING ACCOMPANIED BY A LOCAL COULD ALSO BE AN ADVANTAGE. WE'LL ADAPT OUR APPROACH ACCORDING TO THE SITUATION.

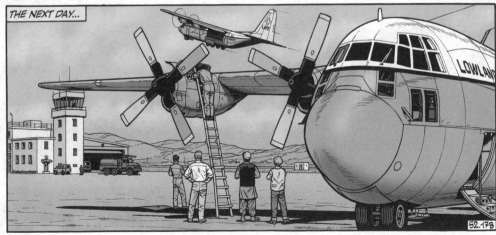

THE NEXT DAY...

52.17B

HOW'S IT LOOKING, BART?

I HAVEN'T FOUND IT... I'M GOING TO DO SEVERAL GROUND TESTS WITH DIFFERENT SETTINGS. THAT'LL TAKE ALL DAY!

WELL... IN THE MEANTIME, WE'LL GO TO THE WORKSHOP TO SEE IF THE EQUIPMENT WOULD ALLOW US TO DO A STANDARD ENGINE SWAP ... AND IF SO, TO ASK FOR AUTHORISATION TO DO SO.

IF IT'S MANNED BY THE SAME GUARD DOG, I'M AFRAID YOU'LL BE WASTING YOUR TIME TALKING!

HEY-Y-Y! ANYBODY THERE?

52.18A

NO ONE...

ASIDE FROM THE TAIL ASSEMBLY WHICH WILL HAVE TO REMAIN OUTSIDE, THIS HANGAR IS BIG ENOUGH TO BRING OUR PLANE IN. IT'S GOT ALL THE EQUIPMENT NEEDED TO MAKE THE NECESSARY REPAIRS.

THERE'S A DOOR LEADING TO THE NEXT HANGAR AT THE BACK. MAYBE WE COULD CHECK IF ANYONE'S THERE?!

ASIM, COULD YOU ASK IF ANYONE'S AROUND?

کسی اینجاست؟

YA-AVL

چه خبره؟!

YA-AVL

WHAT IS IT?

WHAT?... YOU AGAIN, YOU DANGED LITTLE TEXAN? I THOUGHT I TOLD YOU THIS WAS PRIVATE PROPERTY!

52.18B

IT'S MY BOSS HERE WHO WANTED TO TALK TO YOU...

YES. ARE YOU THE HEAD MECHANIC?

THAT'S ME, YES. WHAT DO YOU WANT?

WE MAY HAVE TO DO A STANDARD ENGINE SWAP ON OUR AIRCRAFT IN A FEW DAYS, IN WHICH CASE I WANTED TO ASK IF WE'D BE ABLE TO USE YOUR WORKSHOP ... FOR A FEE, OF COURSE!

OH... WELL... I'LL HAVE TO ASK MANAGEMENT. WE'LL GET BACK TO YOU SOON. YOU SHOULD GO NOW. WE'VE GOT WORK TO DO!

ASIM... YOU'RE FREE TO GO FOR TODAY IF YOU WISH.

MY WORK AS A GUIDE STOPS WHEN YOU'RE AT YOUR HOTEL AND STARTS AGAIN WHEN YOU RETURN HERE. I'LL TAKE YOU BACK WHENEVER YOU WANT — AND I DON'T MIND MAKING A SECOND TRIP FOR YOUR ENGINEERS.

ALL RIGHT, BART?

I DID SOME TUNING UP. I'M GOING TO RUN A TEST...

I'LL GO WITH YOU. BOB, ASIM, WATCH WHETHER IT'S STILL SMOKING...

52.19A

SOON...

SO, DID YOU SEE THE BUFFALO?

AFFIRMATIVE. BUT THERE'S NO EVIDENCE SO FAR THAT IT'S JENKINS'. WE'D NEED A CLOSER LOOK, PREFERABLY FROM INSIDE — BETTER STILL, TO SEE A PLAQUE WITH THE SERIAL NUMBER...

WOULD YOU LIKE ME TO BUDDY UP TO MY MECHANIC BROTHER?

NO. FIRST, I DOUBT YOU'D GET ANY RESULTS. AND SECOND, CONSTANT ATTEMPTS TO GO NEAR THAT PLANE WILL EVENTUALLY MAKE SOMEONE SUSPICIOUS... WE HAVE TO FIND ANOTHER WAY!

LATER...

GOODNIGHT, ASIM. SEE YOU TOMORROW.

THERE'S A MESSAGE FOR YOU, MR HARRISON...

?!

THAT DIDN'T COME FROM FAR — IT'S ON HOTEL STATIONERY!

52.19B

'...CORDIALLY INVITED TO DINNER TONIGHT IN THE DIRECTORIAL SUITE ON THE TOP FLOOR,' SIGNED: 'ABDALLAH CHAZNI. SHOULD YOU BE UNABLE TO ATTEND, PLEASE...'

AND OF COURSE IT'S JUST FOR YOU! IT'S ALWAYS ABOUT THE BOSSES, HERE!

WHILE I GO TO THAT DINNER, YOU HEAD TO THE BAR ... IN CASE EMCEE IS BACK.

IF HE IS, I'M WILLING TO TRY TO GET HIM TO SPILL HIS GUTS — BUT I REFUSE TO DRINK ANOTHER DROP OF WHISKY!

D'YOU THINK THAT...?

I BETCHA I WON'T NEED IT TO GET HIM TO TALK... TACT AND SUBTLETY — YOU'LL SEE!

52.20A

THAT EVENING...

MY DEAR MR HARRISON, I HAVE GREAT ADMIRATION FOR YOU AND YOUR TEAM...

BADGHIS

YOU VOLUNTEERED TO HELP US SO CHARITABLY, EVEN CONSIDERING THE DANGERS INHERENT IN FLYING OVER MOUNTAINOUS TERRAIN WHERE REBEL BANDS COULD TARGET YOU...

NOT ENTIRELY CHARITABLY, SIR... OUR COMPANY KEEPS ITS FEES AS LOW AS POSSIBLE, BUT WE DO GET PAID... PEANUTS, CERTAINLY, BUT WE ALL NEED TO EAT!

52.20B

IT DOES YOU GREAT CREDIT!... MORE TEA?

PLEASE.

I HEARD THAT YOUR AIRCRAFT WAS GROUNDED BECAUSE OF AN ENGINE MALFUNCTION... FOR HOW LONG, DO YOU THINK?

THAT WILL DEPEND ON HOW SERIOUS THE PROBLEM IS. MOST LIKELY WE'LL HAVE TO HAVE AN ELECTRONIC CONTROL UNIT ANALYSED BY A SPECIALISED WORKSHOP IN KARACHI, WHICH COULD TAKE A WEEK...

...AND, WORST-CASE SCENARIO, IF WE HAD TO SWAP THE ENGINE, WE COULD BE GROUNDED FOR TWO WEEKS ... ASSUMING WE'RE EVEN ALLOWED TO USE THE AIRFIELD'S ON-SITE REPAIR SHOP.

DON'T WORRY ABOUT THAT PART. THE WORKSHOP IS OWNED BY MY OWN EMPLOYER, AND I CAN ASSURE YOU THAT SHOULD YOU NEED IT, YOU WILL RECEIVE FULL ACCESS.

AH! THANK YOU — YOU'VE JUST LIFTED A WEIGHT FROM MY SHOULDERS!

Francis Bergese

52.20C

SAY... COME TO THINK OF IT... YOU COULD FIND YOURSELF IDLE FOR A LENGTHY PERIOD OF TIME...

?...

HOW WOULD YOU FEEL ABOUT SOME WORK ON THE SIDE?

?...

MY EMPLOYER, WHO RUNS AN IMPORT-EXPORT COMPANY, ALSO OWNS A SMALL AIR TRANSPORT COMPANY... BUT HE'S SHORT ON PILOTS. YOU COULD CREW SOME FLIGHTS FOR HIM, ON AN AD HOC BASIS, AND YOU'D BE FREE TO RETURN TO YOUR HUMANITARIAN MISSION AS SOON AS YOUR AIRCRAFT WAS AVAILABLE AGAIN.

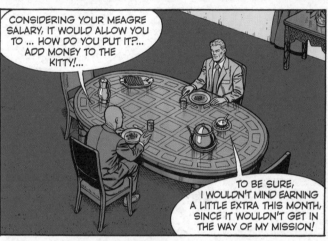

CONSIDERING YOUR MEAGRE SALARY, IT WOULD ALLOW YOU TO ... HOW DO YOU PUT IT?... ADD MONEY TO THE KITTY!...

TO BE SURE, I WOULDN'T MIND EARNING A LITTLE EXTRA THIS MONTH, SINCE IT WOULDN'T GET IN THE WAY OF MY MISSION!

GIVE ME 24 HOURS. MY ENGINEER IS STILL TRYING TO FIND A QUICK FIX... MY ANSWER WILL DEPEND ON HIS FINAL DECISION...

BADGHIS

THINK ABOUT IT. IT COULD PROVE VERY LUCRATIVE FOR YOU!

52.21A

LATER...

BADOM!

COME IN! IT'S OPEN!

SO, EMCEE WAS HERE!

YEP!... HIC!

YOU SAID YOU WOULDN'T DRINK ANOTHER DROP OF WHISKY!

I CHANGED TACT... HIC! BUT I KEPT MY WORD: NOT A DROP OF WHISKY...

...ONLY GIN!...

WELL?

HE'S LEAVING TOMORROW FOR ONE OF THOSE PROFITABLE SPECIAL TRANSPORTS... HIC!... A MISSION WITH NO FLIGHT PLAN THAT IN-VOLVES SNEAKING ACROSS A BORDER...

52.21B

THAT'S IT? WHERE IS HE PICKING UP HIS CARGO? WHICH BORDER IS HE CROSSING? THAT WASN'T WORTH COMING BACK IN THIS CONDITION!

ESPECIALLY SINCE WE ROLLED DICE FOR THE TAB... HIC!... AND HE WON!

WELL... ANYWAY, OUR PLAN IS WORKING: I'VE BEEN RECRUITED, AND HOPEFULLY I'LL BE TAKING PART IN ONE OF THOSE SPECIAL FLIGHTS SOON.

HEY! WE'VE BEEN RECRUITED!

THAT REMAINS TO BE NEGOTIATED... WE'LL TALK ABOUT IT TOMORROW!

THE NEXT AFTERNOON, TUMB AND HIS CREW ARE BACK WITH ANOTHER SHIPMENT...

SO, THAT ENGINE?

WHEN YOU GO BACK TO KARACHI, WE'LL GIVE YOU AN ELECTRONIC CONTROL BOX TO TAKE TO A WORKSHOP FOR ANALYSIS.

WHAT WILL YOU DO IN THE MEANTIME?

I'VE BEEN ASKED TO DO SOME TRANSPORT JOBS WITH A LOCAL AIRCRAFT. I HAVE TO GIVE THEM AN ANSWER TONIGHT.

WHY NOT?!... I'D GO FOR IT. WHAT DO YOU THINK, ASIM?

IF YOU PROMISE TO BE CAREFUL AND TO BE AVAILABLE ONCE YOUR AIRCRAFT HAS ITS ENGINE BACK!

THAT EVENING, AFTER BUCK RETURNS FROM ANOTHER MEETING WITH THE HOTEL DIRECTOR...

I MANAGED TO CONVINCE HIM TO HIRE BOB, TOO, ALTHOUGH IT TOOK TIME. HE KEPT INSISTING THE FLIGHT ENGINEER USUALLY TAKES THE COPILOT'S PLACE...

DID YOU MENTION THOSE TRANSPORT JOBS THAT EMCEE CALLS 'SPECIAL' – WITH A FAT BONUS?

YES... HE LOOKED SURPRISED AT FIRST, THEN HE LAUGHED!...

HA! HA! HA! GOOD OLD EMCEE HAD TOO MUCH TO DRINK AGAIN!

CONSIDER ME INTERESTED, WHAT WITH THE PROMISE OF A NICE BONUS!...

SO YOU BELIEVED HIM!

HE DIDN'T SEEM TO COMPLAIN ABOUT HIS SITUATION.

RIGHT... FIRST I MUST WARN YOU: THE MAN WHO PAYS FOR THESE... ER... SPECIAL JOBS IS SOMEONE VERY POWERFUL AROUND HERE. ANY SLIP, ANY LEAK COULD BE CENSORED IN THE MOST ... PERMANENT MANNER... MAKE SURE YOUR COPILOT UNDERSTANDS...

AS FOR THE BONUS, WE WILL NOT BE GETTING ONE EACH, BOB, OLD BUDDY! WE'LL HAVE TO SHARE!

THE NEXT DAY...

SAFE DROPS, CHAPS! BOB AND I ARE GOING TO GET ACQUAINTED WITH OUR PART-TIME WORK PLANE!

LOWLAND AIR PARTNERSHIP

MY FRIENDS, BEFORE YOU GO, EVEN THOUGH WE SHOULD ALL MEET AGAIN TONIGHT, I'D LIKE TO GIVE YOU MY PHONE NUMBER. IF YOU ENCOUNTER THE SLIGHTEST PROBLEM, DON'T HESITATE TO CALL ME!

52.23A

CELL PHONES WORK AROUND HERE?

SATELLITE PHONES, YES. I MUST BE ABLE TO CONTACT MY SUPERIORS AT ALL TIMES IN CASE OF DIFFICULTIES.

A LITTLE LATER...

HERE'S YOUR MACHINE... GO TO THE COCKPIT AND GET TO KNOW THE CONTROLS. THE BUFFALO SHOULDN'T PRESENT ANY PROBLEMS WHATSOEVER FOR C-130 PILOTS...

DO YOU HAVE THE MANUALS AND THE FLIGHT LOGS?

THE MANUALS ARE ON THE PILOT'S SEAT. AS FOR THE LOGS, I KEEP THEM MYSELF. I HAVE YOUR NAMES — I'LL WRITE THEM DOWN.

تلفن با تو کار داره!

PHONE CALL FOR YOU!

SOME 15 MINUTES LATER...

OK... IT'S EASY ENOUGH!... I STILL HAVE A FEW THINGS TO CHECK IN THE MANUAL...

I'D LIKE TO PEEL THIS LABEL OFF!

52.23B

THE PREVIOUS REGISTRATION NUMBER MUST BE UNDERNEATH!

THE TWO PILOTS HAVE BEGUN A FULL INSPECTION OF THE AIRCRAFT WHEN...

TAKE YOUR SEATS, GENTLEMEN. WE'RE LEAVING!

YOU'RE RIGHT... WE'LL TAKE THE MANUAL BACK TO THE HOTEL AND TRY TO REMOVE THE LABEL WITH STEAM.

TO DO SOME PRACTICE? TAXI AROUND THE RUNWAYS?...

NO TIME... AN URGENT MISSION!

WE'RE SUPPOSED TO PRACTICE TODAY... MR CHAZNI TOLD ME...

?!

MR CHAZNI ISN'T YOUR EMPLOYER — HE'S JUST A MIDDLEMAN. I GOT A PHONE CALL FROM THE BOSS HIMSELF!

WHAT ABOUT OUR KITS? OUR LICENSES? OUR FLIGHT LOGS?

IT'S JUST A DAY TRIP, AND YOU WON'T BE NEEDING YOUR LICENSES.

SOON...

MAKE YOUR HEADING 95 AND STAY AT VERY LOW ALTITUDE. I'M GOING TO SHOW YOU OUR DESTINATION ON THE MAP...

YA-AVL

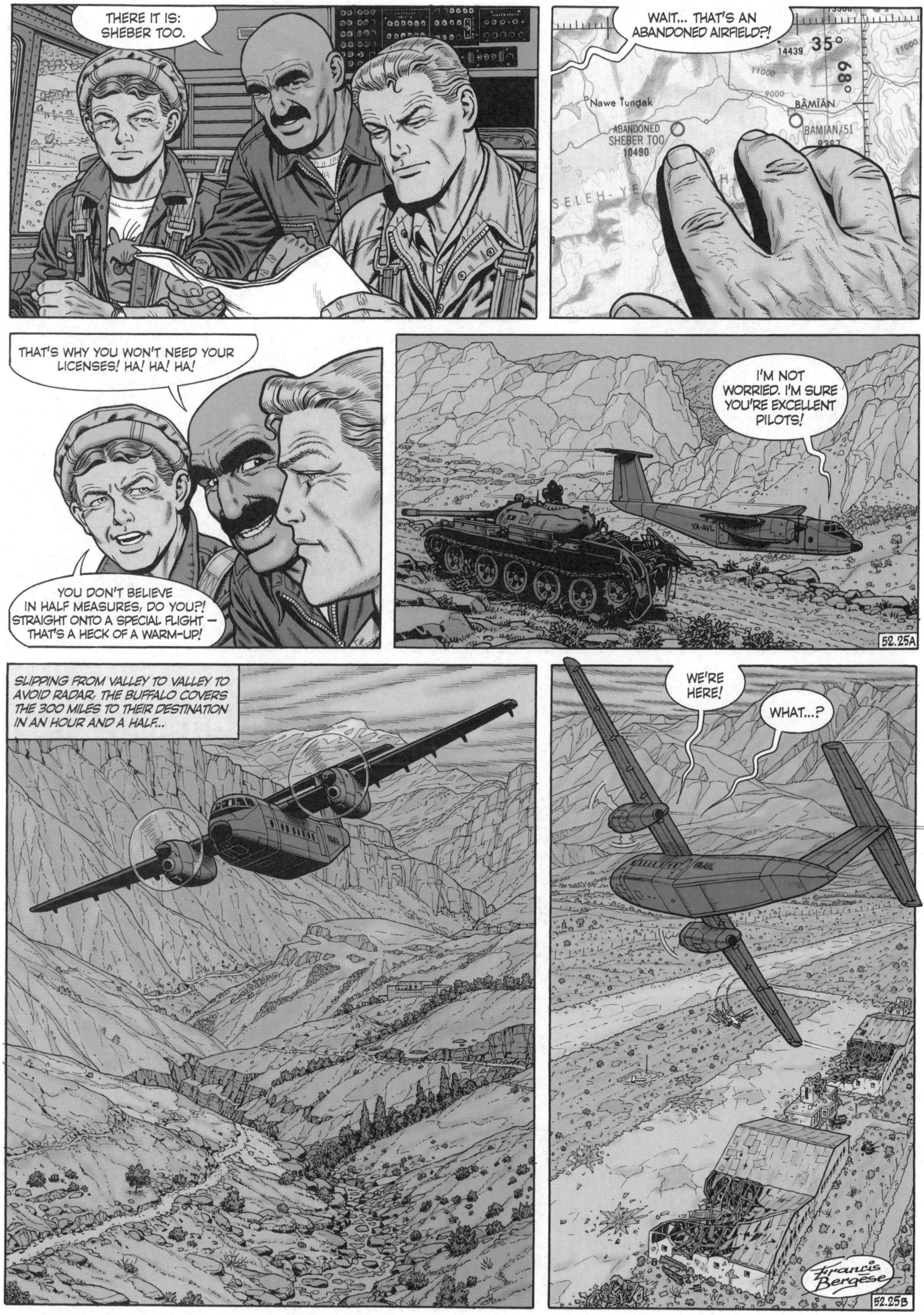
THERE IT IS: SHEBER TOO.
WAIT... THAT'S AN ABANDONED AIRFIELD?!
ABANDONED SHEBER TOO 10490
BAMIAN
THAT'S WHY YOU WON'T NEED YOUR LICENSES! HA! HA! HA!
YOU DON'T BELIEVE IN HALF MEASURES, DO YOU?! STRAIGHT ONTO A SPECIAL FLIGHT — THAT'S A HECK OF A WARM-UP!
I'M NOT WORRIED. I'M SURE YOU'RE EXCELLENT PILOTS!
YA-AVL
52.25A
SLIPPING FROM VALLEY TO VALLEY TO AVOID RADAR, THE BUFFALO COVERS THE 300 MILES TO THEIR DESTINATION IN AN HOUR AND A HALF...
WE'RE HERE!
WHAT...?
Francis Bergèse
52.25B

LANDING'S ON QFU 06* AND THERE'S A VERY STRONG CROSSWIND... SO WATCH IT: DON'T GET BLOWN OFF THE RUNWAY LIKE THAT MORON EMCEE. SOME AREAS AROUND THE STRIP ARE STILL MINED!

*RUNWAY AXIS ORIENTED 60° FROM THE NORTH

BE CAREFUL, KEN!

BOB, OLD FELLOW, ARE YOU CALLING MY ABILITIES INTO QUESTION!?

MASTERFULLY, BUCK PROCEEDS TO LAND THE TWIN-ENGINED AIRCRAFT ON ITS LEFT WHEELS, KEEPING THE WINGS TILTED TO COUNTER THE CROSSWIND...

52.26A

DID YOU SEE WHAT I SAW?

YES... A SMASHED ANTONOV 26 THAT WENT OFF THE RUNWAY!

THERE. PIECE OF CAKE!

TAXI TO THE RAMP... YOU CAN STOP IN FRONT OF THE HANGAR WHERE THAT GROUP OF MEN IS.

SOON AFTERWARDS, THE BUFFALO IS PARKED BEFORE THE HANGAR. THE DOORS ARE OPENED...

HERE'S AHMED, EMCEE'S ENGINEER. HE'LL BE COMING BACK WITH US.

SALAAM ALAYKUM!

52.26B

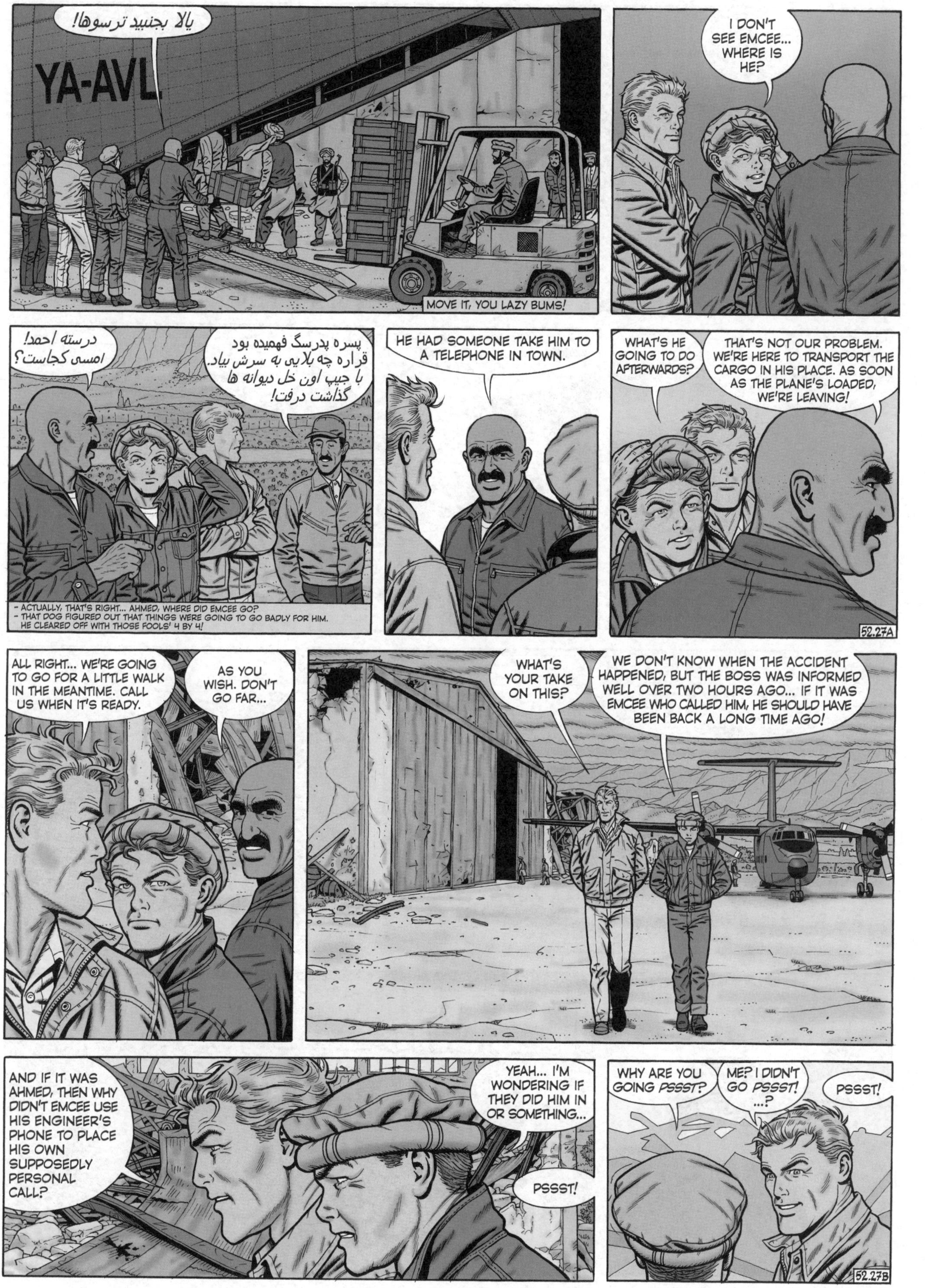

یالا بجنبید ترسوها!
YA-AVL
MOVE IT, YOU LAZY BUMS!
I DON'T SEE EMCEE... WHERE IS HE?
درسته احمد! امسی کجاست؟
پسره پدرسگ فهمیده بود قراره چه بلایی به سرش بیاد. با جیپ اون خل دیوانه ها گذاشت درفت!
- ACTUALLY, THAT'S RIGHT... AHMED, WHERE DID EMCEE GO?
- THAT DOG FIGURED OUT THAT THINGS WERE GOING TO GO BADLY FOR HIM. HE CLEARED OFF WITH THOSE FOOLS' 4 BY 4!
HE HAD SOMEONE TAKE HIM TO A TELEPHONE IN TOWN.
WHAT'S HE GOING TO DO AFTERWARDS?
THAT'S NOT OUR PROBLEM. WE'RE HERE TO TRANSPORT THE CARGO IN HIS PLACE. AS SOON AS THE PLANE'S LOADED, WE'RE LEAVING!
52.27A
ALL RIGHT... WE'RE GOING TO GO FOR A LITTLE WALK IN THE MEANTIME. CALL US WHEN IT'S READY.
AS YOU WISH. DON'T GO FAR...
WHAT'S YOUR TAKE ON THIS?
WE DON'T KNOW WHEN THE ACCIDENT HAPPENED, BUT THE BOSS WAS INFORMED WELL OVER TWO HOURS AGO... IF IT WAS EMCEE WHO CALLED HIM, HE SHOULD HAVE BEEN BACK A LONG TIME AGO!
AND IF IT WAS AHMED, THEN WHY DIDN'T EMCEE USE HIS ENGINEER'S PHONE TO PLACE HIS OWN SUPPOSEDLY PERSONAL CALL?
YEAH... I'M WONDERING IF THEY DID HIM IN OR SOMETHING...
PSSST!
WHY ARE YOU GOING *PSSST*?
ME? I DIDN'T GO *PSSST*! ...?
PSSST!
52.27B

GOOD LORD!

EMCEE!

GO TO HIM. I'M GOING BACK TO THE PLANE. IF ANYONE ASKS, I'LL TELL THEM THAT NATURE HAD A PRESSING CALL FOR YOU!

NICE TO SEE YOU AGAIN, NEIGHBOUR!

YOU OLD DOG! I WAS WONDERING WHERE YOU'D GONE!

THE ACCIDENT WASN'T MY FAULT. THE RIGHT BRAKES DIED ON ME... POOR MAINTENANCE — BUT THOSE FREAKING MECHANICS WILL NEVER ADMIT IT!

ARE YOU HURT?

A BULLET IN THE ARM... AFTER WE GOT OUT OF THE PLANE, I HAD A STRONG FEELING THAT THEY WERE GOING TO DO SOMETHING TERMINAL TO ME. THEIR JEEP WAS NEARBY, ENGINE RUNNING AND NO ONE IN IT...

52.23A

...I JUMPED BEHIND THE WHEEL AND VAMOOSED. THAT'S WHEN I GOT HIT...

I DIDN'T GO FAR AT ALL. AS SOON AS I WAS ABLE TO HIDE THE VEHICLE, I CAME BACK ON FOOT...

ARE YOU NUTS?!

I WOULDN'T HAVE GONE FAR ANYWAY... TOO EASILY SPOTTED! THOSE GUYS HAVE EYES EVERYWHERE...

I CAME BACK BECAUSE DURING A PREVIOUS FLIGHT HERE, I LOOKED AROUND THE HANGARS AND FOUND AN OLD ANTONOV AN-2. IN BAD SHAPE, BUT APPARENTLY AIRWORTHY, WITH A LITTLE FUEL IN ITS TANKS...

52.23B

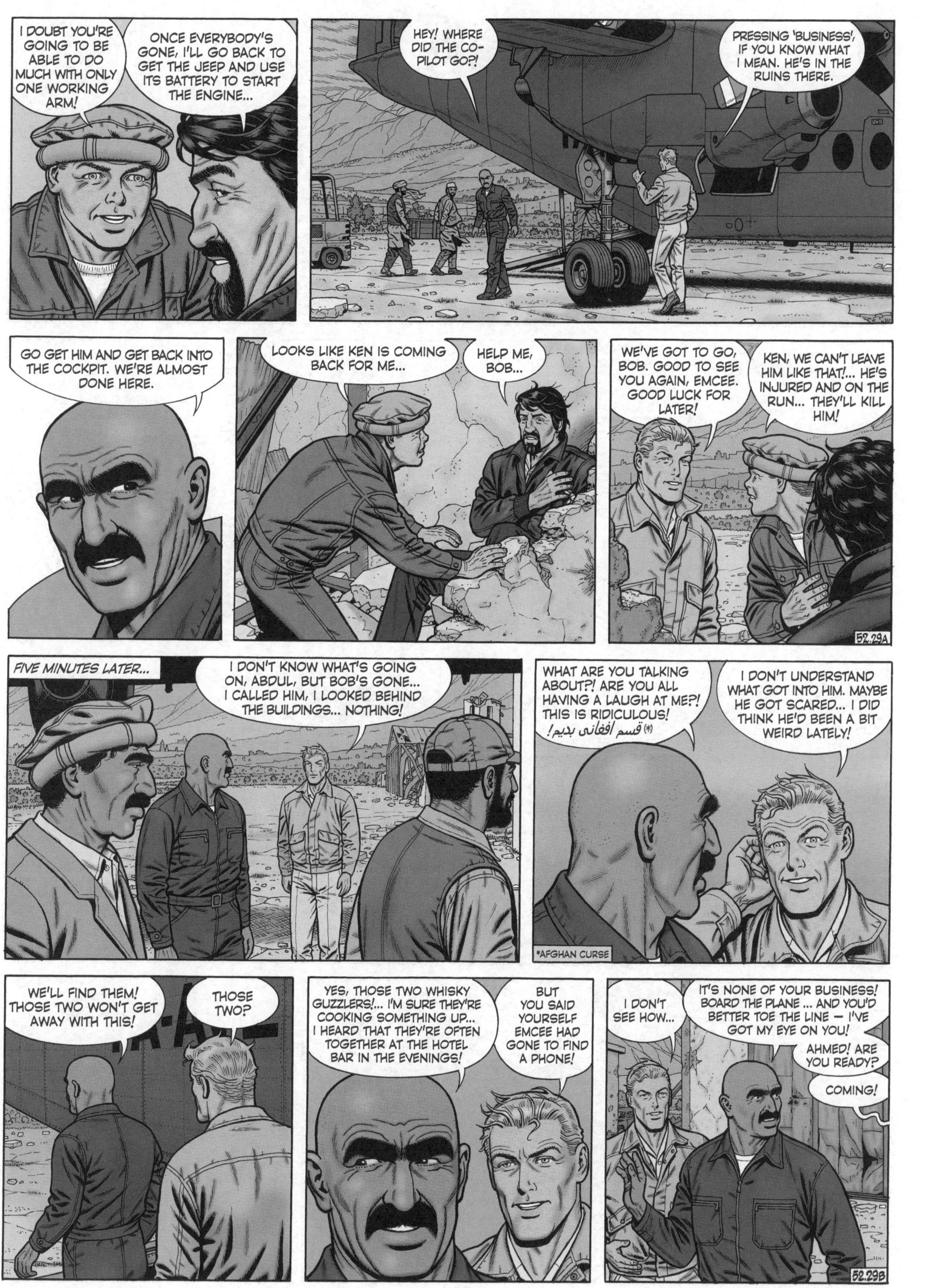
I DOUBT YOU'RE GOING TO BE ABLE TO DO MUCH WITH ONLY ONE WORKING ARM!
ONCE EVERYBODY'S GONE, I'LL GO BACK TO GET THE JEEP AND USE ITS BATTERY TO START THE ENGINE...
HEY! WHERE DID THE CO-PILOT GO?!
PRESSING 'BUSINESS', IF YOU KNOW WHAT I MEAN. HE'S IN THE RUINS THERE.
GO GET HIM AND GET BACK INTO THE COCKPIT. WE'RE ALMOST DONE HERE.
LOOKS LIKE KEN IS COMING BACK FOR ME...
HELP ME, BOB...
WE'VE GOT TO GO, BOB. GOOD TO SEE YOU AGAIN, EMCEE. GOOD LUCK FOR LATER!
KEN, WE CAN'T LEAVE HIM LIKE THAT!... HE'S INJURED AND ON THE RUN... THEY'LL KILL HIM!
52.29A
FIVE MINUTES LATER...
I DON'T KNOW WHAT'S GOING ON, ABDUL, BUT BOB'S GONE... I CALLED HIM, I LOOKED BEHIND THE BUILDINGS... NOTHING!
WHAT ARE YOU TALKING ABOUT?! ARE YOU ALL HAVING A LAUGH AT ME?! THIS IS RIDICULOUS! قسم افغانی بدیم! (*)
I DON'T UNDERSTAND WHAT GOT INTO HIM. MAYBE HE GOT SCARED... I DID THINK HE'D BEEN A BIT WEIRD LATELY!
*AFGHAN CURSE
WE'LL FIND THEM! THOSE TWO WON'T GET AWAY WITH THIS!
THOSE TWO?
YES, THOSE TWO WHISKY GUZZLERS!... I'M SURE THEY'RE COOKING SOMETHING UP... I HEARD THAT THEY'RE OFTEN TOGETHER AT THE HOTEL BAR IN THE EVENINGS!
BUT YOU SAID YOURSELF EMCEE HAD GONE TO FIND A PHONE!
I DON'T SEE HOW...
IT'S NONE OF YOUR BUSINESS! BOARD THE PLANE ... AND YOU'D BETTER TOE THE LINE — I'VE GOT MY EYE ON YOU!
AHMED! ARE YOU READY?
COMING!
52.29B

AS SOON AS THE BUFFALO HAS LEFT THE GROUND, IT TURNS WEST...

ARE WE RETURNING TO QALA I NAW?

THAT'S RIGHT. AND USING THE SAME ROUTE THROUGH LOWER VALLEYS. YOU'D BETTER MAKE SURE WE DON'T GET DETECTED AND INTERCEPTED.

CONSIDERING I'M A HUMANITARIAN AID PILOT, BEING CAUGHT TRAFFICKING ARMS WOULD BE QUITE DETRIMENTAL TO MY CAREER!

I REALLY DON'T LIKE YOUR SENSE OF HUMOUR!... WHO TOLD YOU IT WAS WEAPONS?

A LOOK AT THE CRATES WAS ENOUGH — THANKS FOR CONFIRMING IT!

YOU'RE REALLY STARTING TO ANNOY ME, MR HARRISON! I'VE ALWAYS HATED LIMEYS* ANYWAY!... SO WATCH YOUR STEP, DO YOUR JOB AND SHUT YOUR MOUTH!

*INSULTING TERM FOR ENGLISH PEOPLE

52.30A

MEANWHILE...

IS EVERYONE IN?

YEAH, LET'S GO!

WE NEED TO GET SOME MORE VEHICLES AND SEARCH THE WHOLE AREA. EITHER WE FIND THOSE TWO YANKEES REAL SOON OR WE'RE GOING TO BE IN SERIOUS TROUBLE!

GOOD... I HOPE THEY'RE ALL ON IT. LET'S GO!

A LITTLE LATER...

WE'RE LUCKY THERE WAS A TOOLBOX IN THE JEEP. I DON'T KNOW HOW WE'D HAVE REMOVED THE BATTERIES TO CHANGE THEM OTHERWISE!

THE TYRES ARE FLAT AND WE DON'T HAVE AN AIR PUMP.

52.30B

IF THE ENGINE GIVES US FULL POWER — ASSUMING IT EVEN STARTS — WE OUGHT TO BE ABLE TO TAKE OFF ANYWAY.

AS FOR THE LANDING, BETTER NOT THINK ABOUT IT NOW!

GETTING CLOUDY!

WHAT DOES IT MATTER?

WE'RE FLYING UP A VALLEY THAT ENDS IN A PASS OVER 8,000 FEET HIGH...

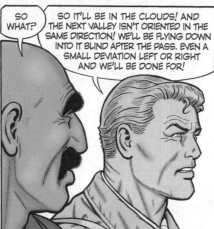

SO WHAT?

SO IT'LL BE IN THE CLOUDS! AND THE NEXT VALLEY ISN'T ORIENTED IN THE SAME DIRECTION! WE'LL BE FLYING DOWN INTO IT BLIND AFTER THE PASS. EVEN A SMALL DEVIATION LEFT OR RIGHT AND WE'LL BE DONE FOR!

YOU... YOU WON'T DEVIATE, THAT'S ALL!

THE IMPORTANT THING IS TO MARK THE EXACT MOMENT WE CREST THE PASS AND TURN QUICKLY INTO THE HEADING THAT'LL LET US DESCEND ALONG THE NEW VALLEY'S AXIS.

BUT ... WILL YOU BE ABLE TO DO IT?!

WITH YOUR HELP, YES. YOU'LL READ ME THE HEADING OFF THE COMPASS SO I CAN FOCUS ON PRECISE MANOEUVRING.

WE COULD TURN BACK AND LOOK FOR A DIFFERENT ROUTE...

TOO LATE. THE VALLEY'S TOO NARROW NOW. WE'RE OUT OF OPTIONS!

JUST A QUICK PUSH OF THE STARTER TO SEE IF THE PROPELLER WILL TURN...

BRBRRAOW

ALL RIGHT!... NOW ALL WE HAVE TO DO IS CLEAR THE DEBRIS AND OPEN THE HANGAR DOORS!

THIS IS IT!

AT OUR CURRENT SPEED AND CLIMB RATE, IT'LL TAKE US EIGHT SECONDS TO REACH THE TOP OF THE PASS FROM THE MOMENT WE ENTER THE CLOUD COVER...

1... 2...

HEADING 313...

52.32A

313...

4... 5...

...6... 7...

THREE ONE TH... THREE...

CRESTING THE PASS NOW!

THREE... AH... ONE THREE!

OK... HERE GOES NOTHING!

HEADING, ABDUL!

ER... 309... 306...

52.32B

34

THREE OH FO... THREE...

LEVELLING OFF!

FAIRLY SOON, THE CLOUD COVER PARTS, AND...

ALLAH IS GREAT!

EACH OF YOU LOOK OUT A SIDE... IF YOU SEE A MOUNTAIN WALL, YELL!

THE RELIEF BECOMES LESS PRONOUNCED UP AHEAD... IT SHOULD BE EASY FLYING FROM HERE ON!

AT THAT MOMENT...

WROOAARRRR

52.33A

HERE WE GO!

GIVE THE ENGINE SOME TIME TO WARM UP!

IT'LL WARM UP ON THE WAY TO THE RUNWAY... I HAVE NO INTENTION OF WAITING AROUND HERE!

BARELY OVER A MINUTE LATER...

WATCH THAT NASTY CROSSWIND!

ESPECIALLY WITH FLAT TYRES AND BRAKES THAT HAVE ALMOST GIVEN UP THE GHOST... IT MAKES FOR SLOPPY TAXIING!

52.33B

FULL THROTTLE... LET'S HOPE THE ENGINE HOLDS!

...AND EVERYTHING ELSE!

LABORIOUSLY, SHAKING FROM NOSE TO TAIL, THE OLD AIRCRAFT BEGINS PICKING UP SPEED...

THIS'LL DO... WITH HER LARGE RUDDER, THIS CRATE GETS GOOD YAW CONTROL. READ ME THE ASI*, EMCEE!

*AIRSPEED INDICATOR

IT'S IN KILOMETRES PER HOUR... 45... 48...

52.34A

...55... 58... 60...

FLLLPOLOP

WHAT THE...? SHE'S GONNA SHAKE HER-SELF APART!

BRROOMM

THE TYRE'S COME OFF!

NROOOM

WE'RE ACTUALLY MAKING BETTER SPEED! 70... 80...

AS LONG AS THE STRIP IS FLAT... CROSS YOUR FINGERS THAT THERE AREN'T ANY HOLES!

52.34B

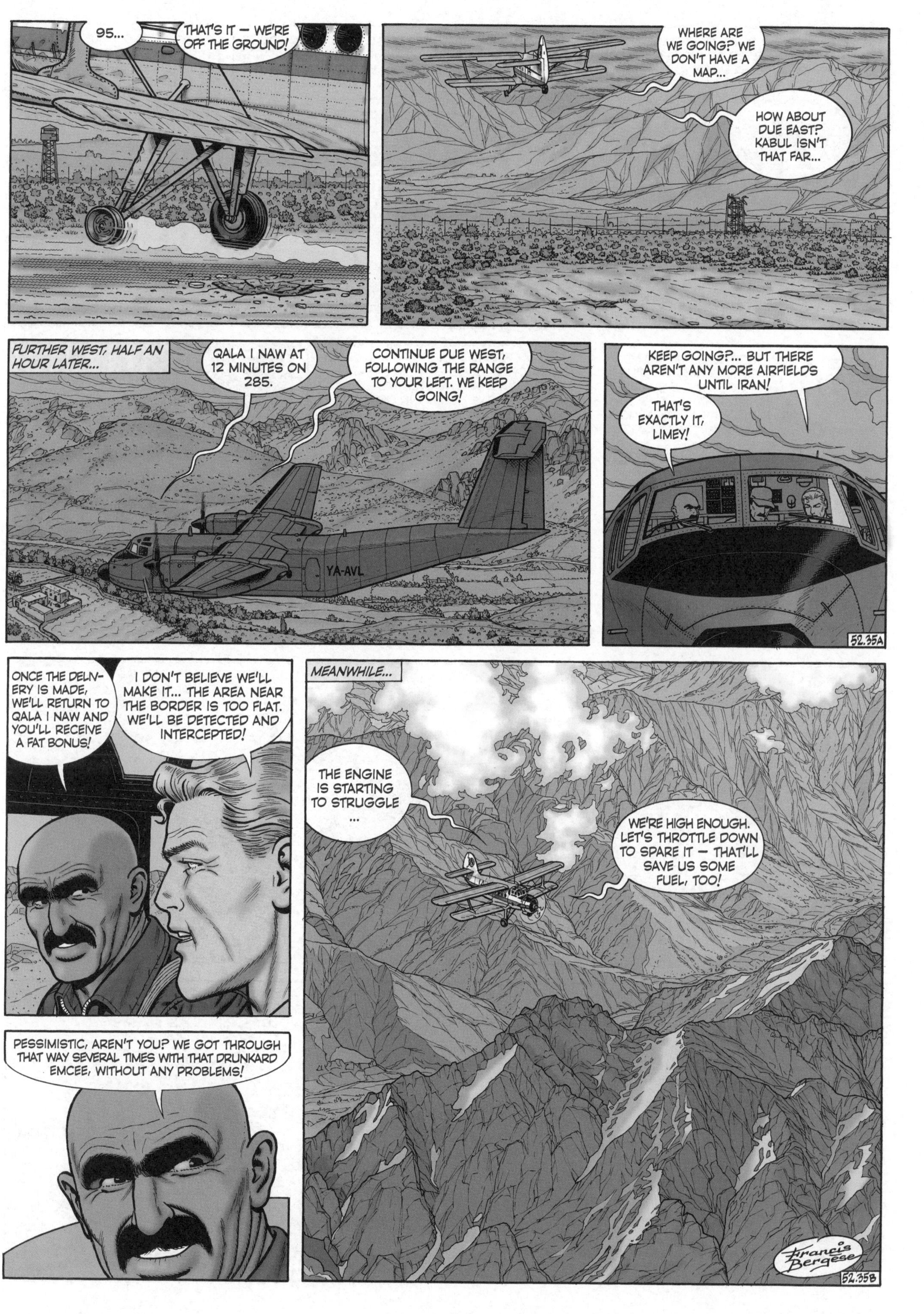
95...
THAT'S IT — WE'RE OFF THE GROUND!
WHERE ARE WE GOING? WE DON'T HAVE A MAP...
HOW ABOUT DUE EAST? KABUL ISN'T THAT FAR...
FURTHER WEST, HALF AN HOUR LATER...
QALA I NAW AT 12 MINUTES ON 285.
CONTINUE DUE WEST, FOLLOWING THE RANGE TO YOUR LEFT. WE KEEP GOING!
YA-AVL
KEEP GOING?... BUT THERE AREN'T ANY MORE AIRFIELDS UNTIL IRAN!
THAT'S EXACTLY IT, LIMEY!
52.35A
ONCE THE DELIVERY IS MADE, WE'LL RETURN TO QALA I NAW AND YOU'LL RECEIVE A FAT BONUS!
I DON'T BELIEVE WE'LL MAKE IT... THE AREA NEAR THE BORDER IS TOO FLAT. WE'LL BE DETECTED AND INTERCEPTED!
PESSIMISTIC, AREN'T YOU? WE GOT THROUGH THAT WAY SEVERAL TIMES WITH THAT DRUNKARD EMCEE, WITHOUT ANY PROBLEMS!
MEANWHILE...
THE ENGINE IS STARTING TO STRUGGLE ...
WE'RE HIGH ENOUGH. LET'S THROTTLE DOWN TO SPARE IT — THAT'LL SAVE US SOME FUEL, TOO!
Francis Bergese
52.35B

SO, EMCEE... NOW THAT WE HAVE BOUND OUR FATES FOR BETTER OR WORSE ... I'M THINKING YOU'RE MORE LIKELY TO ANSWER A QUESTION THAT WOULD HAVE BEEN AWKWARD BEFORE...

GO ON, OLD BUDDY! YOU SAVED MY LIFE... I WON'T KEEP ANY SECRETS FROM YOU!

HAVE YOU MET OR HEARD ABOUT A PILOT NAMED JENKINS? HE WAS DOING HUMANITARIAN FLIGHTS ON A BUFFALO...

...A BUFFALO THAT KEN AND I THINK IS THE SAME ONE WE FLEW TO SHEBER TOO TO PICK UP THE WEAPONS...

HMMM?... AND WHAT DO YOU WANT WITH THIS JENKINS?

LISTEN... AT THIS POINT, MIGHT AS WELL LAY OUR CARDS ON THE TABLE. JENKINS WAS... OR IS... A CIA AGENT INVESTIGATING AN ARMS TRAFFICKING RING...

...AND MY FRIENDS AND I ARE A COUPLE OF THROWN-TOGETHER HUMANITARIAN CREWS, SENT BY THE PENTAGON'S SPECIAL OPERATIONS COMMAND OFFICE TO LOOK FOR JENKINS.

I'M JENKINS.

52.36A

WH... WHAT?!... COME AGAIN?

I'M TELLING YOU THAT I'M JENKINS!

TH... THAT'S NOT POSSIBLE!... BEFORE WE LEFT, WE WERE GIVEN A FILE TO READ THAT INCLUDED PHOTOGRAPHS OF ALL THREE OF THE BUFFALO'S CREW. ONE OF US, AT LEAST, SHOULD HAVE RECOGNISED YOU THE MOMENT WE MET!

A BROKEN NOSE, LONG HAIR AND A BEARD WILL CHANGE A FACE...

OK, SPILL!

SOON AFTER WE ARRIVED, AS WE WERE ABOUT TO LEAVE TO MAKE SOME DELIVERIES IN THE NORTH, WHERE WE HADN'T FLOWN YET, OUR GUIDE SELIM SHOWED UP WITH A RUSSIAN WE'D MET BEFORE...

I DON'T KNOW THE AREA YOU'RE GOING TO VERY WELL, SO FEDOR, WHO'S A PILOT FOR BADGHIS AIR SYSTEM, OFFERED TO COME ALONG.

52.36B

IT TURNED OUT TO BE A HIJACKING... SOME TIME INTO THE FLIGHT, THE TWO MEN PULLED OUT GUNS AND FORCED US TO CONTINUE FLYING TO A NEIGHBOURING COUNTRY: TURKMENISTAN.

JUST PAST THE BORDER, WE LANDED ON A MAKESHIFT AIRSTRIP IN A DESERTED AREA, WHERE SEVERAL VEHICLES FULL OF ARMED MEN WERE WAITING FOR US TO STEAL THE CARGO...

SORRY WE HAD NO TIME TO GET TO KNOW EACH OTHER BETTER, FRIENDS. GOODBYE!

IT ALL HAPPENED IN A SECOND. EVEN AS I HEARD THE SHOTS THAT KILLED MY PARTNERS, I JUMPED FEDOR AND GRABBED HIS PISTOL IN BOTH MY HANDS. IN THE STRUGGLE, IT WENT OFF ONCE...

BANG

52.37A

FEDOR WAS SHOT THROUGH THE HEART AND DIED INSTANTLY. SEVERAL MEN PILED ON ME AND BEAT ME TO WITHIN AN INCH OF MY LIFE. THAT WAS WHEN A RIFLE BUTT FLATTENED MY NOSE.

I VAGUELY HEARD SELIM PREVENT THEM FROM FINISHING ME OFF. OF COURSE — THEY DIDN'T HAVE A PILOT TO BRING THE PLANE BACK TO THEIR BOSS ANY MORE!

WHEN I BEGAN TO COME TO, THEY'D DRAGGED ME BACK TO THE COCKPIT...

NOW WE'RE GOING BACK TO QALA I NAW!

I WAS AFRAID THEY'D FINISH THE JOB OF KILLING ME ONCE WE ARRIVED ... BUT THEY WERE SHORT ON PILOTS, AND TO MY EVERLASTING SURPRISE, THEY ASKED ME TO REPLACE FEDOR UNDER A NEW IDENTITY. THREATS AND PROMISES, AND SUDDENLY I'M AN ARMS TRAFFICKER!

I COULDN'T HAVE FOUND A BETTER POSITION FROM WHICH TO INVESTIGATE, AND THE DEATH OF MY TEAM WAS AMPLE MOTIVATION. BUT I REFUSED TO FLY THE BUFFALO AGAIN. CUTTING ALL TIES TO THAT PLANE ONLY REINFORCED MY NEW IDENTITY...

52.37B

AND IF THAT ACCIDENT AT SHEBER TOO HADN'T HAPPENED, HOW MUCH LONGER WOULD YOU HAVE KEPT THIS UP?

I WAS UNDER CONSTANT SURVEILLANCE, HAD NO CONTACTS... I KEPT WAITING FOR AN OPPORTUNITY, AND I ALWAYS HOPED I'D PICK UP MORE DETAILS ON THE INS AND OUTS OF THE TRAFFICKING...

YOU HAVE PLENTY FOR A NICE, FAT REPORT, ESPECIALLY WITH KEN'S AND MY TESTIMONIES. I...

WHAT IS IT?...

A MARINE AV-8*! WE'RE BEING INTERCEPTED!

*AMERICAN DESIGNATION FOR THE BRITISH-DESIGNED VERTICAL TAKE-OFF AND LANDING JET HARRIER

52.38A

I BET THEY'RE SAYING ALL KINDS OF NICE THINGS TO US OVER THE RADIO, BUT THIS OLD CRATE DOESN'T HAVE ONE ANY MORE!

THEY'RE PROBABLY GOING TO TAKE US TO BAGRAM BASE, NORTH OF KABUL. WE CAN'T BE FAR FROM IT NOW...

FAR TO THE WEST, ON THE NORTH SIDE OF THE SAFID MOUNTAIN RANGE...

THE BASE AT HERAT IS ONLY 30 MILES TO THE SOUTH...

DON'T WORRY, LIMEY! THESE MOUNTAINS SHIELD US FROM THEIR RADAR!

YOU'RE FORGETTING THAT AN AWACS* COULD SEE US AT ANY TIME. WHAT ARE WE SUPPOSED TO DO IF THEY SEND FIGHTERS AFTER US?

THAT'S NOT GOING TO HAPPEN! WE HAVE OUR INFORMATION – NO AWACS PLANES HAVE TAKEN OFF TODAY!

*DEDICATED RADAR SURVEILLANCE AIRCRAFT

TEN MINUTES LATER, OVER THE HIGH MOUNTAINS NEAR KABUL...

WE'RE BARELY LIMPING NOW. THIS ENGINE IS ABOUT TO CROAK!

52.38B

THESE MUST BE THE LAST MOUNTAINS BEFORE THE KABUL VALLEY... WE HAVE TO GET OVER THEM!

MEANWHILE...

FIVE MINUTES TO THE IRANIAN BORDER...

SEE? THERE WAS NO REASON TO WORRY!

52.39A

OH?... LOOKS LIKE YOU SPOKE TOO SOON!

BROOOOOWWW

قسم افغانی بدیم!

AFGHAN CURSE

I'M SWITCHING THE RADIO TO THE INTERNATIONAL FREQUENCY!

ABSOLUTELY NOT! IGNORE THEM AND KEEP FLYING!

I DON'T THINK THAT'S A GOOD IDEA. WITHOUT A FLIGHT PLAN, WE'RE CONSIDERED INTRUDERS. THEY'LL BE AUTHORISED TO FIRE BEFORE WE REACH THE BORDER!

WE HAVE AN AFGHAN REGISTRA-TION. THEY WON'T SHOOT!

52.39B

I WOULDN'T BET ON IT!

DON'T BET THAT I WON'T SHOOT YOU, EITHER! I KNOW ENOUGH PILOTING TO LAND THIS PLANE SAFELY.

THEY'RE SIGNALLING US TO BANK LEFT ... TOWARDS HERAT. WE SHOULD DO AS WE'RE TOLD!

SHUT UP!

FIVE MORE WORDS: THEY ARE GOING TO FIRE!

52.39C

THAT WAS A WARNING SHOT. THE NEXT ONE WILL BE ON TARGET, AND IF THERE IS ANY AMMUNITION IN YOUR CRATES, WE'LL MAKE A FINE FIREWORKS DISPLAY!

I'M TELLING YOU THEY WON'T DARE! MAKE A SINGLE MOVE TO USE THE RADIO OR CHANGE DIRECTION AND I'LL SHOOT YOU!

I THINK YOU'RE THE ONE WHO WON'T DARE SHOOT! YOU'RE PUTTING UP A SHOW FOR YOUR BOY HERE BECAUSE HE'LL REPORT ON YOUR BEHAVIOUR TO YOUR BOSS ... BUT IF IT WEREN'T FOR THIS WITNESS, WE'D ALREADY BE EN ROUTE TO HERAT!

THE SECOND JET IS BEHIND US AND WILL FIRE ANY SECOND... I'M TURNING!

52.40A

BANG

OW!

Francis Bergese

52.40B

42

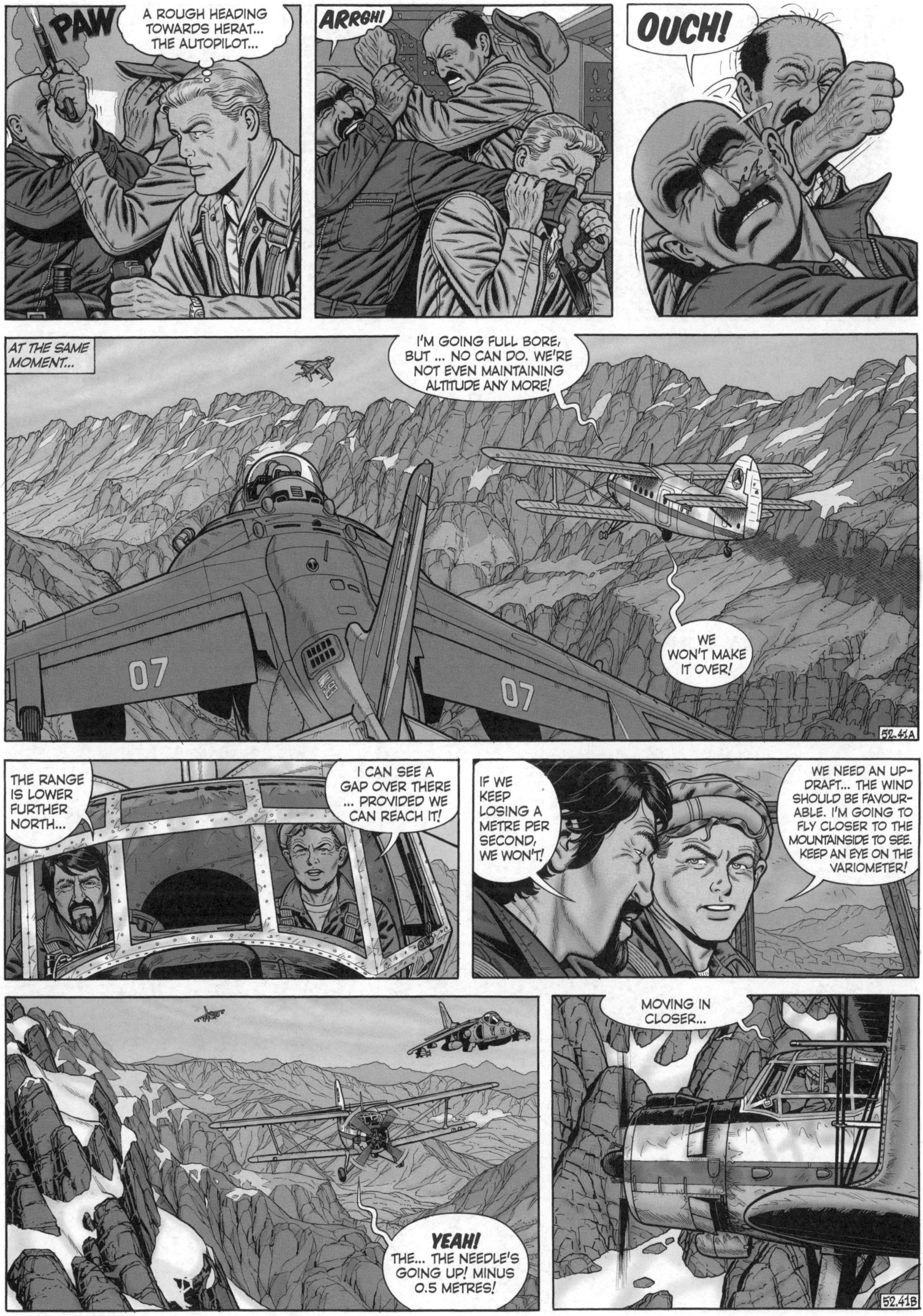
PAW
A ROUGH HEADING TOWARDS HERAT... THE AUTOPILOT...
ARRGH!
OUCH!
AT THE SAME MOMENT...
I'M GOING FULL BORE, BUT ... NO CAN DO. WE'RE NOT EVEN MAINTAINING ALTITUDE ANY MORE!
WE WON'T MAKE IT OVER!
07
07
52.41A
THE RANGE IS LOWER FURTHER NORTH...
I CAN SEE A GAP OVER THERE ... PROVIDED WE CAN REACH IT!
IF WE KEEP LOSING A METRE PER SECOND, WE WON'T!
WE NEED AN UP-DRAFT... THE WIND SHOULD BE FAVOURABLE. I'M GOING TO FLY CLOSER TO THE MOUNTAINSIDE TO SEE. KEEP AN EYE ON THE VARIOMETER!
YEAH!
THE... THE NEEDLE'S GOING UP! MINUS 0.5 METRES!
MOVING IN CLOSER...
52.41B

THAT'S IT! THE RATE OF CLIMB IS POSITIVE!

PLUS 0.2 METRES!

NEARLY AT PLUS ONE METRE... COME ON! COME ON! JUST A BIT MORE!

IT'S GOTTA BE ENOUGH... IT'S ENOUGH!

WATCH OUT — WE'RE ABOUT TO STALL*!

*LOSE TOO MUCH SPEED TO STAY ALOFT

PHEW! I THOUGHT WE WERE GOING TO END UP SPLATTERED ALL OVER THESE ROCKS!

52.42A

NOW WE JUST FOLLOW OUR GUIDE.

FIVE MINUTES LATER...

HE'S SHOWING US THE GRASS STRIP... HE MUST HAVE NOTICED THE STATE OF OUR LEFT WHEEL!

STRAPPED IN TIGHT, ENGINE OFF... PROTECT YOUR ARM, EMCEE!

52.42B

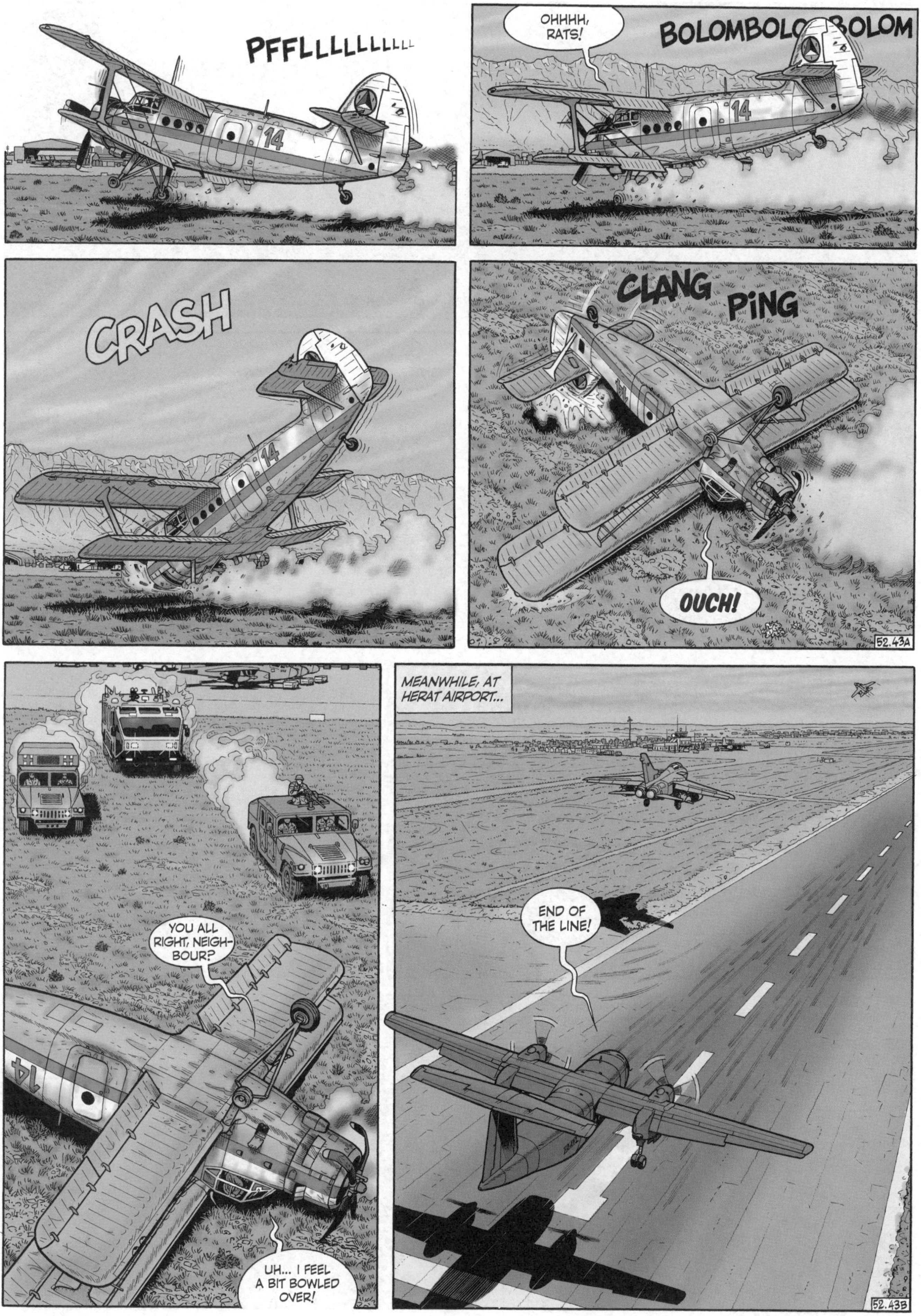

PFFLLLLLLLLLL
OHHHH, RATS!
BOLOMBOLO BOLOM
CRASH
CLANG
PING
OUCH!
52.43A
YOU ALL RIGHT, NEIGH-BOUR?
UH... I FEEL A BIT BOWLED OVER!
MEANWHILE, AT HERAT AIRPORT...
END OF THE LINE!
52.43B

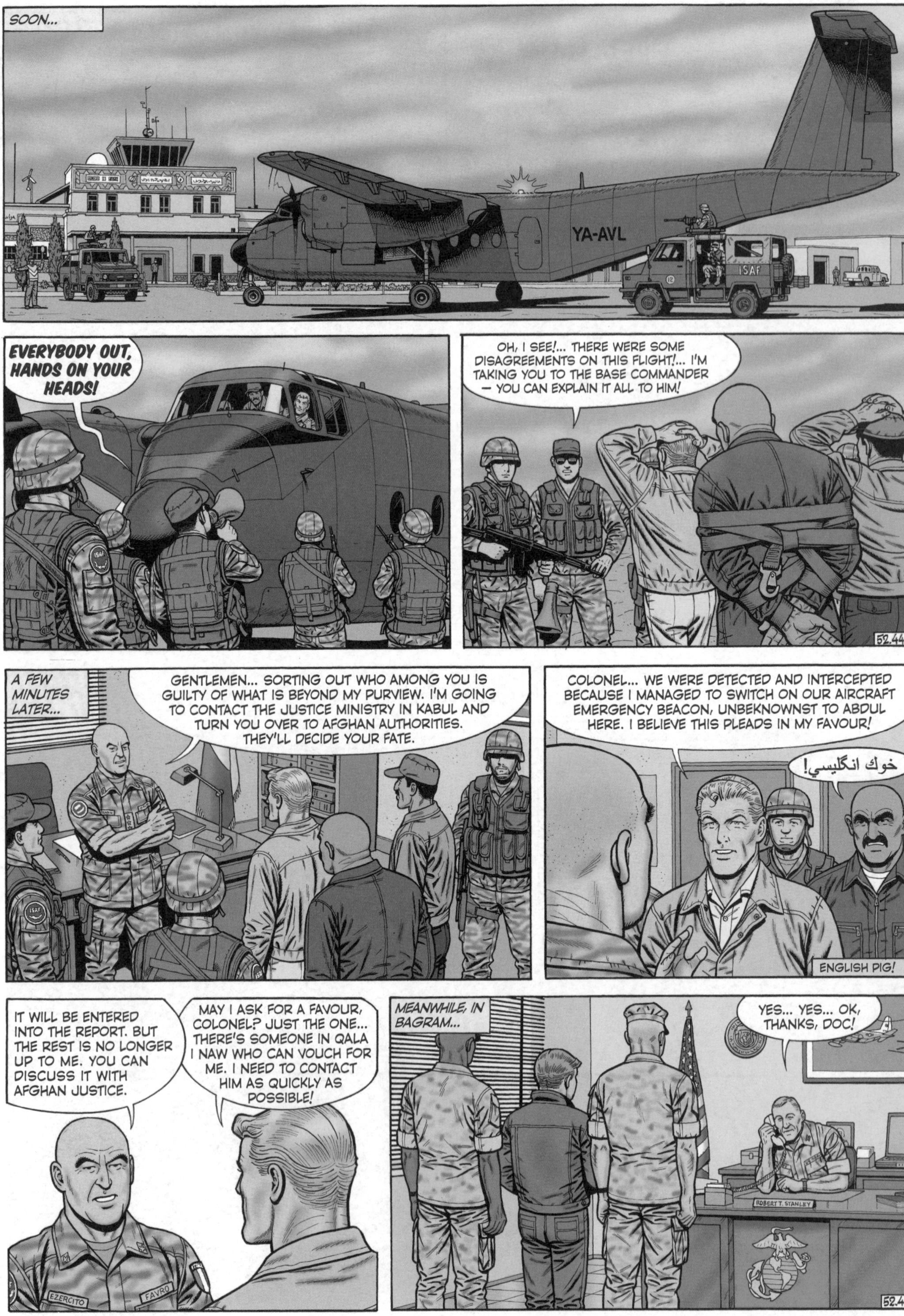

SOON...
YA-AVL
ISAF
EVERYBODY OUT, HANDS ON YOUR HEADS!
OH, I SEE!... THERE WERE SOME DISAGREEMENTS ON THIS FLIGHT!... I'M TAKING YOU TO THE BASE COMMANDER – YOU CAN EXPLAIN IT ALL TO HIM!
A FEW MINUTES LATER...
GENTLEMEN... SORTING OUT WHO AMONG YOU IS GUILTY OF WHAT IS BEYOND MY PURVIEW. I'M GOING TO CONTACT THE JUSTICE MINISTRY IN KABUL AND TURN YOU OVER TO AFGHAN AUTHORITIES. THEY'LL DECIDE YOUR FATE.
COLONEL... WE WERE DETECTED AND INTERCEPTED BECAUSE I MANAGED TO SWITCH ON OUR AIRCRAFT EMERGENCY BEACON, UNBEKNOWNST TO ABDUL HERE. I BELIEVE THIS PLEADS IN MY FAVOUR!
خوك انگليسي!
ENGLISH PIG!
IT WILL BE ENTERED INTO THE REPORT. BUT THE REST IS NO LONGER UP TO ME. YOU CAN DISCUSS IT WITH AFGHAN JUSTICE.
MAY I ASK FOR A FAVOUR, COLONEL? JUST THE ONE... THERE'S SOMEONE IN QALA I NAW WHO CAN VOUCH FOR ME. I NEED TO CONTACT HIM AS QUICKLY AS POSSIBLE!
EZERCITO
FAVRO
MEANWHILE, IN BAGRAM...
YES... YES... OK, THANKS, DOC!
ROBERT T. STANLEY

YOUR FRIEND IS BEING SEEN TO BY THE BASE SURGEON. IT WAS A CLOSE CALL, BUT HE'LL RECOVER THE USE OF HIS ARM.

RIGHT... LET'S GO BACK TO YOUR RIDICULOUS STORY!... YOU SAY YOU'RE IN AFGHANISTAN TO TRANSPORT HUMANITARIAN AID, THEN SUDDENLY YOU FIND YOURSELF AN ARMS TRAFFICKER AGAINST YOUR WILL ON AN ABANDONED AIRFIELD, AND YOU ESCAPE IN A DECOMMISSIONED ANTONOV AN-2!...

THAT'S IT, SIR... MORE OR LESS!

I DON'T BELIEVE A WORD OF IT!... ASIDE FROM THE CONDITION THE ANTONOV IS IN!... DID YOU THINK I'D LET YOU WALK OFF THIS BASE AS IF EVERYTHING WERE NORMAL?!

WELL, YES... I HAVE TO RETURN TO QALA I NAW AND RESUME MY HUMANITARIAN FLIGHTS!

SERIOUSLY? DO I LOOK THAT STUPID TO YOU?!

YOU'RE A CIVILIAN, SO WE'LL TURN YOU OVER TO AFGHAN AUTHORITIES. THEY'LL FIGURE OUT WHAT TO DO WITH YOU.

NO! NOT THAT! I'LL TELL YOU EVERYTHING.

BUT WE NEED TO BE ALONE... IT'S IMPORTANT, SIR.

FINE... LEAVE US, MARINES.

52.45A

MY NAME IS CAPTAIN TUCKSON, US AIR FORCE. I'M HERE ON A MISSION FOR THE PENTAGON'S SPECIAL OPERATIONS COMMAND...

THAT'S IT! THIS TIME I'M GOING TO...

PLEASE, SIR, PLEASE! CONTACT GENERAL SCOTT AT SPEC-OPS!...

...AND TELL HIM THAT THE MISSION IS A SUCCESS. WE FOUND JENKINS!

WHO'S JENKINS?

THE FELLA IN YOUR OPERATING ROOM!

THE NEXT DAY, ON THE PARKING LOT AT HERAT AIRPORT...

HELLO, KEN!

ASIM! AM I GLAD TO SEE YOU HERE! I WAS WONDERING WHAT TROUBLE I WAS HEADING INTO!

52.45B

THE END

The author wants to thank for their kind assistance: Jean-Luc Béghin, Armand Billault, François Bousseau, Jean-Marc Brûlez, Marc Chassard, 2/61 Transport Squadron 'Franche-Comté', Yvan Fernandez, Alain Guérin, Didier 'Higgins' Leroux, Denis Mercier and Ali Rahimi. With a special mention for Lise, his proof-reader, eraser, secretary, receptionist, moral support and patient wife.